THE UGLY ANIMALS

THE UGLY ANIMALS
We can't all be pandas

SIMON WATT

The
History
Press

First published 2014

The History Press
The Mill, Brimscombe Port
Stroud, Gloucestershire, GL5 2QG
www.thehistorypress.co.uk

British Library Cataloguing in Publication Data.
A catalogue record for this book is available from the British Library.

ISBN 978 0 7509 6058 8

Typesetting and origination by The History Press

CONTENTS

THE UGLY ANIMAL PRESERVATION SOCIETY

THE UGLY ANIMAL Preservation Society is a comedy event with a conservation twist and was the starting point for this very book. The society was founded by biologist, writer and TV presenter Simon Watt and is dedicated to raising the profile of some of Mother Nature's more aesthetically challenged children. In September 2012 they teamed up with the National Science and Engineering Competition to initiate a world-wide poll that saw the blobfish voted the ugliest animal in the world.

The society performs all over Britain, aiming to share their love of the wild world through the medium of stand up and their line-ups have featured a range of comedians including Paul Foot, Chris Dunford, Helen Arney, Bec Hill, Dean Burnett, Dan Schreiber, Ellie Taylor, Suzi Ruffell, Sarah Bennetto, and Iszi Lawrence.

Their first show was held in London in October 2012 and since then they have performed all over the country, including the Edinburgh Science Festival, Bristol Big Green Week, the Green Man Festival and the Cheltenham Science Festival. Details of their future shows and further information can be found at www.uglyanimalsoc.com.

INTRODUCTION

THE PANDA MADE me do it. It seems a strange excuse, but it is true.

Pandas are wonderful creatures. They exude a monochrome charisma that has made them famous the world over. The poor giant panda has seen its numbers plummet as human settlement and industry has encroached more and more on its habitat. Without breeding programmes and the protection of the bamboo forests where it lives, it could become extinct. Having said that, it may be endangered, but at least it is loved. It has become the poster boy for conservation and its cute and cuddly face can be seen adorning everything, from lunchboxes to Italian cars. Charities have rallied to its aid and it has become a national symbol of China. A large portion of its success has come from its evolutionary good fortune to happen to look like a teddy. The majority of endangered species are not so lucky. Many are incapable of grabbing headlines. In the limelight, many do not have star potential. But the catastrophe befalling the natural world is so much bigger than being a matter of saving the eye-catching species that star in documentaries. We should not pick and choose what survives, based solely on our shallow sense of aesthetics. The problems facing our planet are much bigger than that.

EXTINCTION

Extinction is a natural phenomenon. We can go further and say that extinction is an essential component of evolution: it is fundamental to the survival of the fittest. In order for natural selection to work, some species must succeed while others must die. We would not be here today if it were not for the demise of the dinosaurs. Extinction prunes the tree of life and research suggests that perhaps 99.99 per cent of all species that have ever lived have gone extinct. The average species only hangs around for about 5 or 10 million years. In many ways, we humans are merely filling our time, waiting our turn to disappear. Though extinction is an ongoing process, there have been spikes in its rate, known as the 'mass extinctions'. We think that there were five particularly dangerous periods when the majority of species went under, the worst of which happened 250 million years ago and is known as 'the great dying'. No one can be certain what caused it: it may have been an eruption from a super volcano or even a giant asteroid that whacked the earth, but it wiped out 95 per cent of all species and life is lucky to have survived at all.

Extinction may well be a natural phenomenon, but it is currently happening at an alarming rate. We estimate that mankind has accelerated the rate of extinction to between 1,000 and 10,000 times higher than it should be. Scientists refer to this man-made massacre as 'the sixth great extinction'. It can be hard to believe that we are as potent a force of extinction as an asteroid strike, but it seems that we are.

THE SPICE OF LIFE

The variety of life is truly awe-inspiring. We estimate that there are around about 8.7 million species, of which less than 2 million have been formally described. We seem to discover about fifty species a day, with the majority of these being insects. A new species of beetle is discovered every few hours.

We tend to be mammal-centric and almost narcissistic in our love of nature: we only care about species that remind us of ourselves, or those we consider cute. We favour animals with big eyes and bushy tails. We prefer our animals to have, at the very least, recognisable faces. Insects tend to be viewed as icky, and yet they are the majority. This is one of the reasons why we have to stop being so shallow in our superficial views of eco-systems. If many creatures disappeared without a trace tomorrow, I doubt the world would notice and many species may even prefer it. If a few key invertebrates vanished, it could cause global calamity, or at the very least smash our human society. Flies aren't pretty, but they pollinate our crops. The lifestyle and jobs of detritivores – species that live on faeces – are unappealing, but without them we would be up to our neck in it. We may well find about fifty species a day, but we estimate that up to 200 species are disappearing daily too.

ENDANGERED BUT NOT UGLY

We have all heard of the plight of the snow leopard, the elephant, the rhino, the mighty lion, the polar bear and the gorilla. It is a tragedy that some of these species could well die out within our lifetime. It is dreadful to think that we could one day have to explain to our children what a tiger was. We call these species the 'charismatic megafauna' and they grab the headlines. These are the animals that we all learn about and learn to love from childhood. There have always been people proclaiming that we must save the whale, but until now, no one has shouted, 'Save the slug'. Even our zoos seem to have a bias, favouring creatures that will draw in the crowds, as opposed to those that make our skin crawl.

UGLY BUT NOT ENDANGERED

There are many amazing species out there that are not as well known as they should be, simply because of their dreadfully unattractive looks. The naked mole rat is a fascinating creature, with a queen and a caste system akin to that of ants and bees. It looks like a sabre-toothed sausage and it is studied the world over because of its long lifespan, inability to feel pain and resilience to cancer. Its appearance makes it a perfect candidate for this book but, fortunately, its population is stable in the wild and its safety is assured, because of the specimens maintained for study in medical research laboratories and zoos the world over. The greater short-horned lizard is a species I find fascinating, because of its highly unusual anti-predator defence technique of shooting blood from its eyes at any assailants. Though its population is declining in some parts of the world, it is sufficiently widespread to mean that limited conservation money would be wiser spent elsewhere. The same goes for the floating cartilaginous head that is the sunfish and the terrifyingly unsightly goblin shark. They are far from pleasing to the eye, but conservationists class them as of least concern. We do not sing the praises of species like these enough, but they are secure and do not need our consideration as badly as others. They are, for now at least, not at risk of going extinct. I want this book to focus on species that need our attention and help as much as the panda does. I wanted to find the ugly ambassadors for all the neglected endangered animals that have been overlooked because of their appearance.

UGLY BUT DATA DEFICIENT

Trying to focus on endangered species has proven to be a more difficult task than I had originally envisaged. This is mainly because the vastness of the natural world poses conservationists with substantial logistical problems. The International Union for the Conservation of Nature is the leading authority on the state of the planet's wildlife. It is striving to document and determine where each species lives and how its population is faring. This is a gargantuan task and the result is that, for many animals, we have no idea about the size and distribution of their population. Not only does this mean that it is likely that many species are disappearing without us ever having noticed their existence in the first place, but that many species we are aware of may be doing much worse than we know. When we uncover a new species in some of the world's diversity hot spots, the chances are that it is endangered because of its small and limited range. We can guess that it is rare and in need of protection, even if we have not yet formally recognised its rarity. The long-tailed ninja slug, which fires love darts at its mate, was only recently discovered in the heart of Borneo. Like so many creatures found in this region, it is still awaiting formal classification, but the chances are that it will go straight onto the endangered species list. Scientists are trying to protect these areas, knowing that any damage done could irreparable.

Lack of knowledge is a problem we also have with the animals that live in the depths of the sea. Many of these regions are so unexplored that we know next to nothing about the wildlife that lives down there. For instance, there are so many forms of cephalopods, the family that features squid and octopus, that look hideous enough to be at home in this book. There is *Vampyroteuthis infernalis*, a deep-sea monstrosity with a biological name that translates as 'the vampire squid from hell' and an appropriately horrifying appearance. There is *Promachoteuthis sulcus*, nicknamed 'the gob-faced squid' because of its strangely human-like mouth. Only a single specimen has ever been found, making it so rare that we are unable to assess its rarity. The vast majority of cephalopods are listed as data deficient; we just don't have the information we need to understand if they need protecting or not. The same goes for the frighteningly fanged denizens of the deep that are the anglerfish: very few of them have had their conservation status determined yet. The Louisiana pancake fish has skin like batter and a flat-as-a-pancake appearance. This bottom-dwelling fish was only discovered in 2010 in the Gulf of Mexico, shortly before much of the area was ruined by the notorious Deepwater Horizon oil spill. The impact of the oil and dispersants on the region's deep-sea species is poorly understood, but it seems likely that the batfish

and many other strange species could well be under threat without us even knowing.

The focus of this book is on species that are both in some way ugly and in some way endangered. I have aimed for a light and comic tone, because conservation is too important to be above a little satire. Furthermore, the issues raised in conservation can be depressing; it can feel like every time you look up biology in the news, you are only checking what has died today. I think that we must savour the world's wackiness while we can. We must celebrate our conservation successes when we have them and we must marvel at all of life. Being sensible and austere is not the only means of communicating a conservation message.

I hope this book shows that, like beauty, ugliness is only in the eye of the beholder: that, just because a species is aesthetically challenged, its plight should not be overlooked. Some of the world's weirdest-looking creatures are marvellous precisely because of their awful anatomy. It is their massive nose, funny face or off-kilter colour pattern that makes them so special.

I have nothing against the panda, but it already has its champions. The animals in this book don't. Every species alive is an ongoing evolutionary experiment and is in some way interesting. We simply have to look more closely.

THE UGLY ANIMALS

AYE-AYE

(*Daubentonia madagascariensis*)

IN SOME PARTS of Madagascar, the local people harbour a fearful dread of the aye-aye and so kill it on sight. They regard glimpsing it as, at best, a sign of bad luck, at worst, an omen of death. Such superstition-inspired violence, combined with the destruction of its forest habitat, has resulted in this remarkable species becoming endangered. Perhaps that is why this highly distinctive and unusual lemur is constantly and rudely flipping everyone the bird: its most noticeable feature is a distinctively long and skinny middle finger.

The aye-aye is a nocturnal tree-dweller found in a range of habitats, from primary rainforest to dry, deciduous forest, on the island of Madagascar. It spends its daylight hours sleeping in an elaborate nest of intertwined twigs and dead leaves, located high up in the crown of tall trees. These nests are far from ramshackle affairs and can take up to twenty-four hours to construct. As individuals move from place to place, they either build new nests or squat in those vacated by other aye-ayes.

It is the largest nocturnal primate and the most evolutionarily distinct of all the lemurs, being the only living representative of the *Daubentoniidae* family of primates. During much of the nineteenth century, it was misclassified as a rodent because of its continuously growing incisors, thick coat of coarse, black hair peppered with longer, white guard hairs, and a sumptuous bushy tail that more than doubles the length of the body. To help see in the dark of night it has large, yellowish, almost startled-looking eyes.

The aye-aye has evolved to fill the niche that is occupied in other parts of the world by species of woodpeckers and squirrels, but which are absent in Madagascar. As such, it has developed some fascinating morphological adaptations. Each of its long and narrow fingers brandishes a curved, claw-like nail. Its third finger is the most impressive in its arsenal, being yet longer and thinner, almost skeletal in appearance. It knocks and taps on tree trunks to see if there are any insect larvae inside. Then, cocking its enormous, bat-like, leathery ears forward, it listens for reverberations within the wood and the tell-tale signs of food squirming around beneath the bark. If it hears anything, it uses its sharp gnashers to gash a hole in the tree and its freaky long finger to probe for prey. Unlike our fingers, which only have hinge joints, the highly dexterous middle finger of the aye-aye has a ball and socket joint, allowing it to swivel nimbly while probing for its fodder. It also uses these amazing anatomical tools to extract flesh from hard fruits such as coconuts and ramy nuts, looking almost like someone using a long spoon to reach the good bits at the bottom of an ice-cream sundae.

'... highly dexterous *middle finger* ...'

IF NIGHTMARES HAD wings, then they would look like the Greater Adjutant. With plumage like dead umbrellas and a beak like a scabbed ice pick, this stork from southern Asia looks like a gangly, balding Goth. Its long, wrinkly neck is adorned with a low-hanging, wizened pouch and surrounded by a messy, almost Elizabethan, ruff. Though it has much darker wings, its body is a miserable, rain-cloud grey and it has a wingspan of well over 2m.

'Their local Indian name … translates as "bone-swallower" …'

The adults stand to attention at nearly 1.5m tall and when they walk, they seem to march. Their species name, adjutant, is a military rank. Their local Indian name, *Hargila*, translates as 'bone-swallower' and is apt for such a large-mouthed scavenger. They swallow bones whole and feast on rotting flesh, and are so revered as scavengers that they were once part of the logo of the Calcutta Municipal Corporation. There are reports from the nineteenth century of them feeding on the partly burnt human corpses disposed of along the funeral Ghats of the Ganges River. Nowadays, they are frequent visitors to city refuse dumps, where finding leftover decaying food is easy. If the opportunity arises, they will take the initiative and kill food of their own. They have been known to attack large insects, frogs, rodents, snakes and small reptiles. Witnesses even attest to them swallowing wild ducks whole.

Like other storks, they lack well-developed vocal muscles and so generally communicate by grunting and clacking their beak. In winter, they congregate to breed in compact colonies that include other species of birds. Males fight for position, seeking the best trees in which to build their large nests. There, the female lays a clutch of three or four eggs, which she and the male take turns to tend. The parents lovingly care for their young, using their expansive wings to shade them from the sun. The adult birds have a more innovative, and disgusting, technique for keeping cool: they poo all over their own bare legs so that the moisture acts like a putrid, cooling balm.

The endangered Greater Adjutant is only found in two small, separate breeding populations in India and Cambodia. It has lost much of its nesting habitat and feeding sites, as suitable wetland habitats have been cleared, drained and polluted with pesticides. In some places they are even hunted, as some still believe an old superstition that the bird carries within its skull a mystical 'snake-stone' that will relieve snake-bites and cure leprosy.

'… the moisture acts like a putrid, cooling balm.'

GREATER ADJUTANT
(*Leptoptilos dubius*)

THE PROBOSCIS ANOLE is commonly known as the 'Pinocchio anole', after the deceitful wooden puppet of lore. It is quite an unfair name, as it must be only the males of this species of lizard that are liars, as the females don't develop the same lance-like snout. The novel nose of the male is probably a sexually selected trait used to intimidate rivals and attract females. It is not the only flashy display that the males use, though: they also use a dewlap. A dewlap is a flap of erectile cartilage that is tucked away, hidden atop the throat of the lizard when it is at rest. When they want to impress, they unfurl this flamboyant fan. In many species of anolis lizard, these flag-like appendages boast bright colours and some even have an extra flap on their back to enhance the effect. Each different species sports its own unique combination of colours and patterns.

There are over 350 different species of anolis. All of them have slim, long-tailed bodies and toes bearing adhesive pads, similar to those found in geckos, which allow them to cling to and climb steep surfaces. Though most are green or brown, some can change colour in line with changes in their temperature or mood. This has led to many being mistaken for the famously changeable chameleons.

'*... will even dabble in* **cannibalism** ...'

The genus is an exceedingly flexible one and has adapted to fill different niches. A subtly different species has evolved to fit in on almost every island or habitat that exists throughout its range. This makes it an important group for biologists who want to unravel the mysteries of evolution, and they study it intently. The green anole has become the first reptile to have its genome sequenced.

This species is a forest specialist and was first discovered in the dense Andean cloud forests of Ecuador in 1953. It was not spotted again after 1960 and so was thought extinct until its rediscovery in 2005. Its range is severely restricted and all observed individuals have been found in only four locations, predominantly in vegetation along a single stretch of road. There is a continuing decline in the quality of its habitat, due to logging, grazing and other human pressures, which is likely to cause further damage to its already diminished numbers, and so it is listed as endangered. It feeds on crickets, spiders, moths and other insects and will even dabble in cannibalism, should it come across smaller lizards.

'*... a sexually selected trait used to* **intimidate rivals** *and* **attract females.**'

PROBOSCIS ANOLE

(Anolis proboscis)

PINK VELVET WORM

(Opisthopatus roseus)

VELVET WORMS ARE inch-long voracious carnivores that like nothing more than feasting on any smaller invertebrates that they might find such as termites, woodlice, small spiders and miniscule molluscs. Velvet worms are the only members of an ancient phylum known as the Onychophora, meaning the 'claw-bearers'. This unusual group has changed little over the last 400 million years and is thought to represent the missing link between arthropods (a group that includes insects and spiders) and annelids (commonly known as segmented worms). There are thought to be about 180 members of the group in total. They are famous among biologists for their unorthodox sex lives and peculiar method of hunting.

Most give birth to live young rather than laying eggs externally, and in most cases the fertilisation is also internal. For this, some species have evolved a penis, while the males of many Australian species exhibit special structures on the head, which apparently take over certain tasks in transferring sperm to the females. In some species, sperm is collected by these structures and the male dives, head first, into the female's reproductive tract.

Sporting soft, flushed flesh adorned with water-repellent scales and tiny, sensitive, hair-tipped papillae, the pink velvet worm is the most dapper of this disgusting brood. Like any fashion-conscious invertebrate, it changes its wardrobe regularly, moulting its plush skin every fourteen days or so.

Though it was once thought extinct, it has been rediscovered in a single forest of South Africa. It likes to live in rotting logs and beneath the leaf litter on the forest floor. Its narrow range, coupled with the destruction of its habitat through logging and the introduction of invasive species, has rendered it critically endangered.

It usually hunts at night, moving slowly through the leaf litter on eighteen pairs of stumpy, unjointed, clawed legs, while searching for prey. Once food is in its sights, it deploys its unusual and distinctive weaponry: its slime cannons. Twin jets of glue-like goo shoot from its face and ensnare its struggling quarry, making resistance futile. It can fire this slime up from a distance of up to 4cm.

'Twin jets of glue-like goo shoot from its face ...'

The slime, which can account for up to 11 per cent of the organism's weight, is mostly made up of water with a dash of sugars and a protein very similar to collagen. The thinness of the jet means the goo dries incredibly quickly, condensing the stringy active ingredients.

Once prey has been rendered immobile by these gloopy lassoes, the worm pierces its victim's flesh and squirts digestive juices directly into the body, breaking down tissues so that it may later slurp them up like a gross, partially digested smoothie. It also eats its used gunge, as it would be a shame to waste it. It takes the pink velvet worm about twenty-four days to restock its awful arsenal of slime and be ready for another shoot-out

IN MANY WAYS the Asian tapir looks like a minimalist elephant. It is as though it had wanted to grow the famous enormous ears and the trunk, but simply couldn't be bothered. The snout might well be short, but it is still a highly versatile tool. It is really a prehensile extension of the upper lip and nose and allows the tapir to grasp and wrench leaves from twigs before stuffing them into its mouth. It can also act like a snorkel while swimming.

The Asian tapir is the largest species of tapir and can grow to be 2m long and weigh up to half a tonne. It is also the most evolutionarily distinct of the five living species of tapir, and the only one surviving in the Old World. Fossil evidence suggests that tapirs are of an ancient lineage and that their closest living relatives are the rhinos. Their form has changed little over the past 35 million years, although the proboscis probably did not develop until relatively recently, at some point in the last few million years. Prehistoric tapirs once roamed Europe, North America and South-east Asia and the fossilised remains of an even larger, giant tapir, called *Megatapirus*, have been excavated in China.

The Asian tapir, unlike its American cousins, bears an idiosyncratic white band on its back and sides. This pattern may act as disruptive camouflage, helping break up the profile of the

'... a minimalist elephant ...'

animal so that predators struggle to spot it in the dim light of the forest. Infants, however, are born with a reddish-brown coat and make the fashion faux pas of covering it with a mix of white stripes and spots.

They are usually shy, solitary creatures, preferring to forage at dusk and at night, using an acute sense of smell and excellent hearing to find their way about. Their eyesight is generally poor and only made worse by the darkness. They mark out large tracts of land as their territory, spraying urine on plants to act like smelly signposts, and prefer to stick to distinct paths that they have bulldozed through the undergrowth. Territories frequently overlap and individuals may communicate using a vocabulary of high-pitched squeaks and whistles.

Fragmented populations occur throughout South-east Asia, including some in Malaysia, Indonesia, Thailand and southern Myanmar. Their numbers have declined by more than 50 per cent in the past forty years, due mainly to habitat loss, as much of their home is converted to palm oil plantations.

'... a vocabulary of high-pitched squeaks and whistles.'

ASIAN TAPIR

(Tapirus indicus)

'... a face that is *acne pink.*'

THE SCIENTIFIC NAME for the northern bald ibis translates roughly as 'the reclusive old man'. If I looked like that, I would want to hide away too. For an animal that looks so drab and dark from the distance, up close it seems almost colourful. The feathers have a hint of blue with a metallic green sheen, while the glossy feathers of the wings have a silken purple hue. It has a long, red, scimitar-like bill and a face that is acne pink.

Unlike most other forms of ibis, the ibis of the Geronticus genus nest on cliffs rather than in trees and prefer arid habitats to the wetlands used by their relatives. The northern bald ibis is a social species foraging in large, loose flocks, looking mainly for lizards and beetles. They feed companionably in groups by pecking at the ground, rooting around in loose, sandy soil or by using their long, curved bill to probe into cracks and fissures in the earth. They have been known to gather together and gorge on locust swarms, killing many of these notorious pests, but the indiscriminate use of pesticides has removed this and other food sources, leading to the birds' disappearance from many regions they used to inhabit.

The northern bald ibis was once widespread across the Middle East, northern Africa and southern and central Europe, but is now confined to two wild populations in Syria and Morocco, with over 95 per cent of truly wild birds concentrated in one subpopulation in Morocco. The Syrian population is migratory, and satellite tagging has shown that at least some members spend their winter holidays in the highlands of Ethiopia before returning south to breed.

The ibis breeds in loosely spaced colonies, nesting on cliff ledges or amongst boulders on steep slopes, usually on the coast or near a river. It starts breeding between 3 and 5 years of age, and seems to pair monogamously for life. The male chooses the best nest site he can find and thoroughly clears it of debris. Then, standing proudly in his bachelor pad, he advertises for a female by waving his crest and giving low and romantic, rumbling calls. Once the birds have paired, the bond is reinforced through bowing displays and mutual preening and they begin construction of a nest using twigs and grass, where the female lays a clutch of two to four rough-surfaced eggs. Both parents share the burden of incubating the eggs and feeding the chicks. It is a long-lived bird, the oldest recorded captive specimen reaching 37 years of age.

Numbers are currently increasing, owing to the efforts of conservationists who, in several locations, are trying to establish semi-wild breeding colonies. The species is currently the rarest bird of the Middle East and is classified as critically endangered.

NORTHERN BALD IBIS

(Geronticus eremita)

KOMODO DRAGON
(*Varanus komodoensis*)

THERE ARE SO many myths about dragons. They do not fly or rise menacingly from the depths of the sea. No, they live on a few islands in Indonesia.

'... a strong *bite* and ... painful *venom*'

St George never even saw one and, if he had, my money would have been on the dragon anyway. For a start, they have a strong bite and a mild but painful venom. A modern myth was that their saliva was rife with bacteria, which would cause their prey to drop dead from septic wounds a few days following an attack. But contrary to this popular belief, recent findings show that the dragon's saliva has no more bacteria than that of any meat-eater that doesn't brush its teeth twice daily. It does eat an extraordinary amount of meat, though, and can consume up to 80 per cent of its body weight in a single sitting.

One myth that does turn out to be true, however, is the one about virgin birth. Several Komodo dragons in zoos have given birth without the need of mating. This method of asexual reproduction is known as parthenogenesis.

In the natural world, there are many different systems for determining the sex of offspring. These include having different numbers or types of chromosomes, or the temperature of the egg. In humans, males are the heterogametic sex, meaning that they have two different sex chromosomes, one called X and the other called Y. Females are homogametic, meaning they have two X chromosomes. For birds and many reptiles, including the biggest lizard, the Komodo dragon, the female is the heterogametic sex and has two different sex chromosomes, one called Z and the other called W. In this case, it is the male that is the homogametic sex, having a pair of Z chromosomes.

Sometimes the unfertilised eggs of Komodo dragons can double the number of their chromosomes, meaning that a mama dragon can have male children made entirely from her own genetic material. Some have suggested that this reproductive adaptation allows a single female to enter an isolated ecological niche (such as an island) and, by parthenogenesis, produce male offspring, establishing a sexually reproducing population. We'd best not get started on the Oedipus myth!

It would be a tragedy if this real-life dragon was to drift into the realms of story, but it is a possibility, as it is considered vulnerable to extinction. The population is estimated to be a mere fraction of the size it was fifty years ago. Causes of this decline are widespread habitat loss, a loss of prey species and hunting. No Komodo dragons have been seen on the island of Padar since the 1970s, the result of widespread poaching of the deer that constitute their chief prey.

'... can consume up to *80* per cent of its *body weight* in a single sitting.'

IF CREEPY CRAWLIES give you the willies, then the giant wetas will make you scream. There are over seventy different types of weta, all of which are found only on the islands of New Zealand. The scientific name of their genus recognises their fearsome size and means 'terrible grasshoppers'.

The heaviest insect yet recorded was a specimen of the Little Barrier Island giant weta, an insect that is now found only on Little Barrier Island in the wild, but was once much more widespread on the mainland too. This massive female was more than 85mm long and weighed 71g, three times heavier than a mouse.

These gargantuan insects may have evolved to be so large through a phenomenon known as island gigantism. Large mammalian carnivores are often absent on islands because the possible size of territories are not large enough to sustain their needs or they simply can't reach them because of the water in the way. In their absence, the ecological niches for large predators can become occupied by other species, which can then grow to be larger than normal. Indeed, the giant wetas may have evolved to their XXL size to occupy a niche very similar to that held elsewhere by mice.

The Cook Strait giant weta can reach up to 70mm long. It lacks wings, so has to put up a fight rather than fly away from predators. Its stout, bulky body comes heavily armoured, with the upper surface covered by a series of thickened, overlapping plates, which bear black markings. It has enormous, strong mandibles and its elongated hind legs have five or six large spines that it brandishes above its head in defence. During the day it conceals itself, taking refuge in grass or leaf litter, emerging at night to feed on the leaves and stems of plants. The male seeks out the significantly larger female to breed, by following her pungent scent and dung pellets. When he finds her, they mate for up to a day before the female lays about 200 eggs in the soft soil and then, exhausted, dies. In spring, the eggs hatch and fully formed juvenile wetas emerge.

The Cook Strait giant weta used to be found on mainland New Zealand as well as many offshore islands, but the introduction of rats and other mammalian predators and the clearance of much of its habitat has meant that its range is now restricted to just a few small, rat-free islands in the Cook Strait. This species, along with many other giant weta species, is considered vulnerable to extinction and so conservationists are doing their best to maintain the pristine nature of their few surviving habitats and trying to introduce them back into some of their historic home ranges.

'... *"fearsome* grasshoppers*"* ...'

COOK STRAIT GIANT WETA

(Deinacrida rugosa)

PROBOSCIS MONKEY

(Nasalis larvatus)

THE PROBOSCIS MONKEY is so named because of the male's particularly enormous and pendulous schnoz. It is the largest nose of any primate, drooping over the mouth and capable of growing to be up to a quarter of the body's length. The precise purpose of the male's immense hooter is debatable, but it is likely to relate to some form of sexual selection and may help enhance the loud honking calls males make to entice females.

They live in mangrove swamps on the island of Borneo. Here, the native peoples used to refer to it as the 'Dutch monkey' because its big hooter and pot belly were said to be akin to the features of the Dutch colonisers. I imagine that both the monkey and the European settlers would have been equally offended by the moniker.

The proboscis monkey mostly feeds on young leaves, supplementing its diet with seeds, fruits, flowers and, very occasionally, meat. Bacteria in its gut aid the breakdown of the plant matter, producing gas and bloating the belly to drum-like proportions. Though it spends most of its life in the trees, it is a good swimmer and even has partially webbed feet. If startled, an entire troop may belly flop into the swamp waters below in an attempt to flee from predators.

'... *a mating dance* that is somewhere between ... *head banging* and *twerking*.'

Groups consist of a single mature male and a harem of around six much smaller females and their young. Adolescent males break off to form rowdy bachelor troops until they grow old enough and big enough to fight and take over their own harem. Females may switch harems several times in their lives and compete for the attentions of the male by performing a mating dance that is somewhere between heavy-metal head banging and twerking. A single offspring is born after a gestation period of nearly six months, and the baby will stay with its mother for the first few years.

The numbers of this king of the mingers have crashed dramatically over the last forty years, thanks to the destruction of its habitat. Vast swathes of the native rainforest of Malaysia and Indonesia have been cleared for timber and to make way for oil-palm plantations. Furthermore, the monkey's habit of forming large, visible, ginger groups by the waterside has made it an easy target for hunters with a taste for monkey meat.

'*The precise purpose of the male's* **immense hooter** *is debatable ...*'

THE SHOEBILL IS so named because of the resemblance its beak bears to items of footwear. The comparison is only accurate if we think of unfashionable footwear. Its beak does not look like a snazzy sneaker or some form of trendy trainer, but instead seems more like a worn, old moccasin or a scabby, antiquated clog. This huge, bulbous bill is straw-coloured with erratic, scratchy, grey markings. No matter what kind of boot the beak most resembles, it can measure up to 24cm and it is ferocious. The sharp edges of the mandibles help the shoebill to decapitate its prey and also to discard any vegetation after prey has been caught. As is the case with pelicans, the upper mandible is robust and ends in a sharp, hooked point. It is a lanky bird and can grow to be 1.5m tall, with a wingspan nearly twice as big, allowing it to soar with ease. The dark-coloured legs are fairly long, ending with exceptionally large feet, perhaps to help this massive bird stay stable while standing on aquatic vegetation when hunting. Its yellow-ringed eyes bear an expression of malice and it has plumage that is the gloomy grey of sadness. When it flies, it looks like a spiteful rain cloud just waiting to break overhead.

Having a walk like a dinosaur and the coloration of a fossil, it is perhaps not surprising that its primitive appearance has baffled biologists since its discovery. It resembles the unrelated groups of storks and pelicans in so many ways, but still has unique, difficult-to-classify characteristics. This has led many to think that the shoebill represents a missing link between these two groups; or it could be that the shoebill's defiantly unorthodox appearance indicates how much it has evolved to occupy a distinct and unusual niche.

Maybe its looks are what prompt it to hunt mostly at night. It prefers to hang around poorly oxygenated water, where fish often have to surface for a gulp of air. There, it will ambush its prey, standing statue-still while waiting, but then attacking with lightning speed and power. Prey is grasped from the water in the bird's sharp, hooked beak, which grips, crushes and pierces in an instant. It will eat anything that fits inside its big mouth and, with a beak so broad, it has a great range of prey including fish, amphibians, water snakes, lizards, turtles, rats, young waterfowl and even young crocodiles.

Although widespread throughout central Africa, the shoebill is considered uncommon and vulnerable. The small population is declining due to habitat destruction and degradation, nest disturbance, increased hunting levels and capture for the bird trade. In many areas, the papyrus swamps where it lives are being destroyed by cattle farming and frequent fires.

SHOEBILL

(*Balaeniceps rex*)

SHOW PITY FOR the big-headed turtle. Its massive cranium is not a sign of arrogance or conceitedness. If anything, it is probably a real headache and inconvenience for the species, as it is so large that the big-headed turtle is unable to retract it into its shell for protection. Instead, it has donned a sort of anatomical helmet in the form of a skull of solid bone that encases the pointed head on all sides. There is an advantage to having such a colossal head though; it means it can have an enormous set of jaws. The sharp and vicious beak of the big head is truly formidable, allowing it to crush the crustaceans and molluscs that it likes to eat. It will also use its beak to defend itself and is capable of amputating a finger or two; it will even use it to grasp bushes to aid climbing up the banks of a brook or stream.

The legs too are protected, by large strong scales, as is the long, thin tail. The tail can be nearly as long as the animal's body and the turtle uses it almost like an extra limb, supporting the weight of the body as it clambers over obstacles. The tail is also used for holding on, like an anchor, in the fast-flowing waters of streams. The shell can be up to 20cm, meaning that, from the tip of its long tail to the end of its enormous head, it can be a huge animal. It is far from being a graceful swimmer and likely prefers to walk along the bottom, sticking to shallow streams. There are a few anecdotal tales of it using its massive mouth and strong tail to climb trees, perhaps on the hunt for snails.

Though it is widespread, being found in Cambodia, China, Laos, Myanmar, Vietnam and Thailand, the species is endangered. This is mainly due to popular demand for it as a pet or as a food, which is surely an uncommon combination. Its scarcity in the wild has led to a greater demand and higher market value. To combat this, there are some turtle farms in both Thailand and China, but the illegal trade still seems to be continuing apace. Though very little is known about the biology of the species, its reproductive rate appears to be very low, with females laying only a few eggs a year. This makes it difficult for their population to recover when individuals are lost.

'Its **massive cranium** *is not a sign of arrogance or conceitedness. If anything, it is probably a real headache ...'*

BIG-HEADED TURTLE

(Platysternon megacephalum)

THE LEPODOPTERA MAKE up a large and famous order of insects that includes all butterflies and moths. There are about 180,000 species in total and many are famous because of their beautiful looks. It is hard to see a butterfly fluttering by and not smile. While some species have wings that are drably coloured and highly camouflaged, the wings of others are bright and garish. The pink underwing moth greedily has both. Its body and legs are a mix of brown and black, while its large, leaf-shaped forewings are a dappled grey that allows it to blend seamlessly with its surroundings when the moth lands on the dark bark of a tree. Hidden under the forewings, though, is a pair of black and hot-pink underwings, flamboyantly fringed with little white spots. All in all, it would be safe to say that the pink underwing moth is quite a pretty animal. Think again though, because in its larval stage it would win the prize for best costume at a Halloween party.

The caterpillar normally keeps its frightening face hidden, preferring to avoid trouble by having the general appearance of a crinkled-up old leaf. But when it knows that it has been rumbled and a predator has located it, it rears up, pulling back its hood to unveil a massive head with a pair of large black pupils, ringed with a blue and yellow iris, and a set of vicious white teeth. It looks like the garb worn by a macabre Mexican wrestler. This appearance has prompted the local people to nickname it the 'big head caterpillar'.

All is not as it seems though, for the eyes are not really eyes and the teeth are not really teeth. In fact, the bulbous 'big head' is actually positioned on the caterpillar's rear end. The whole get-up is but an illusion intended to protect the caterpillar. The development of spots that look like eyes is a common anti-predator defence tactic. In some species they may be used to confuse the predator about which direction their quarry might flee; or they may be used to direct the strike of an assailant to a part of the body less essential to survival than the real head. A flash of these eyespots may even startle a predator by creating the impression of a much larger foe. There are a few species of caterpillar that use their big bumped bums to perform convincing impressions of small venomous snakes.

The pink underwing moth is found in Papua New Guinea, the Solomon Islands, Vanuatu, New Caledonia and Australia, where it is considered endangered. It only lives in subtropical rainforest below an altitude of 600m. It is tightly associated with the *Carronia multisepalea* vine, eating and nesting on it. It is pretty picky and only seems to live on the plant when it takes the form of a collapsed shrub, and not when it grows in an upright form. The Australian government is launching a captive-breeding program to increase the numbers of this costumed caterpillar.

PINK UNDERWING MOTH

(Phyllodes imperialis smithersi)

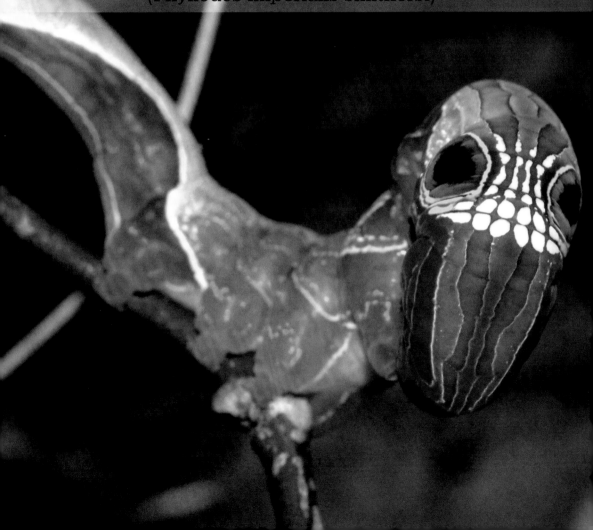

DUGONG

(Dugong dugon)

HISTORIANS THINK THAT the dugong might well be the inspiration behind the mythical creature, the mermaid. Supposedly, lonely sailors would spot them and mistake them for the sirens of Greek legend and so the biological name for their family is the Sirenia. The similarity is hard to fathom; the sailors must have been particularly lonely to find these immense bags of blubber beautiful. Their other name, the sea cow, seems less complimentary, but is much more accurate. These enormous beings graze almost exclusively on sea grass, with an occasional side salad of algae when sea grass is scarce. Together with their cousins, the manatees, they are earth's only herbivorous aquatic mammals.

The dugong is the largest member of this family, growing to about 2.5m in length and weighing about 300kg. There was once a much larger sirenian, the stellar sea cow, which was at least 8m long and weighed several tonnes, but unfortunately this gargantuan brute was hunted to extinction in the eighteenth century, within twenty-seven years of its discovery.

Unlike most other marine mammals, they cannot hold their breath for long periods of time and most dives last a mere minute or so. Surprisingly, the sirenians are not closely related to other marine mammals like whales and dolphins and instead are relatives of the elephant family, sharing a common ancestor with them from around 100 million years ago.

Proponents of the mermaid theory may describe them as graceful, but sluggish might be more apt. Dugongs have a low metabolism and so tend to move relatively slowly. Their average swimming speed is around 10km per hour. Long-distance migration is unknown, but some more sprightly individuals have been recorded swimming up to 600km at certain times of year.

There are historical reports of dugongs gathering in huge herds of thousands. Although they are less abundant today, they are still occasionally seen in groups of 100 or more when food is plentiful. In recent years, when the weather has been particularly cold, manatees have been witnessed huddling for warmth in the waters surrounding nuclear power stations and dugongs may exhibit similar behaviours.

Dugongs are generally seen alone or in pairs. Breeding appears to occur throughout the year, with peak months for births varying geographically. Babies are born in shallow water and must surface almost immediately to take their first breath. The adults, because of their large size, have very few natural predators and have been known to live for more than 70 years in the wild. The species has been traditionally hunted throughout much of its range and though commercial hunting is now banned, many die by becoming accidentally caught and drowned in fishing nets.

'... sailors must have been particularly lonely to find these immense bags of **blubber** beautiful.'

LONG-WATTLED UMBRELLABIRD

(Cephalopterus penduliger)

IN BRAZIL THERE is a frantic form of music often played during carnivals known as *frevo*. The music blares feverishly from saxophones, drums, trumpets and trombones: a mix of marching-band music and jazz. Dancers follow the band, moving rhythmically and acrobatically and often, as is tradition, incorporating swings and gestures with umbrellas as part of their two-step. Maybe this dance is what the male long-wattled umbrellabird is trying its best to emulate.

Males are nearly twice the size of females and sport a large quiff-like crest atop their head and a long, soot-black, feathered wattle that resembles a folded-up umbrella that hangs from the middle of their chest. The wattle can grow to be almost as long as their body. Every morning during the mating season, these males gather around open spaces in the forest known as leks. These focal points act as a clearing-cum-disco and there the males dance and sing in the hope of impressing any ladies who come to watch.

'… like a fat string of morbid tinsel.'

These dances are poorly studied and there is much yet to learn, but it seems that, as part of the dance, the male unfurls his umbrella, inflating his wattle, so that it pumps up in size and the feathers start to splay out, making it look like a fat string of morbid tinsel. Like the *frevo* dancers, it swings, twirls its umbrella and jumps about in an elaborate and exuberant display. Though the bird is usually silent, it also sings during this flamboyant act, making guttural grunting noises and low, booming calls that can be heard up to 1km away.

If the dancing and squawking karaoke is impressive enough, the female will mate with the male and take on the burden of building a nest, incubating the eggs and brooding the chicks entirely by herself. There is some suggestion that the female may store the sperm for many months, to use at a more convenient time, when a good food supply is more guaranteed. They consume large quantities of fruit, and consequently the long-wattled umbrellabird plays an important ecological role within its habitat, helping many plants to disperse their seeds. Though fruit forms the main part of their diet, they are omnivores and, should the opportunity arise, they will also eat large insects, small amphibians and reptiles.

The habitat of this magnificent creature is sadly being destroyed as it is divided by transport infrastructure and decimated by logging, mining and conversion to agricultural plantations. Not only does this loss and degradation destroy the birds' nesting and display sites, but the increased human presence around those that remain may well lead to reduced breeding success. As such, the species is considered vulnerable. Let us hope it will not dance its last tango any time soon.

OK, HAVING A name like 'hagfish' gives you a hint as to just how ugly these chinless wonders are, but it is hard to prepare yourself for their full hideousness. For a start, they don't have jaws and look like a frightful villain from a horror story by H.P. Lovecraft. Their classification has proved difficult and some scientists find them so strange that they are not even certain if they are fish at all. Traditionally, they are grouped together with the other jawless fish, the lamprey, and thought to represent the most primitive group of vertebrates, in spite of the fact that they don't even have a spine. Fossil evidence suggests that they have remained unchanged, and ugly, for the past 300 million years.

> *'... unchanged, and **ugly**, for the past 300 million years.'*

Though they lack jaws, they do still have many hard and sharp teeth made from keratin, the same substance that makes up a rhino's horn and our hair and nails. These lie in two vicious rows along their rasping tongue. They hunt for little invertebrates but prefer to scavenge and the dead bodies of large creatures like whales teem with them. When they come across a rotting carcass they greedily burrow face-first into the flesh, even knotting their tails to generate torque as they grate their way inside their meal. Surrounded on all sides

> *'... they **greedily** burrow face-first into the **flesh** ...'*

by their dinner, they absorb the nutrients directly through their skin; in fact, the hagfish's skin can absorb nutrients even faster than its intestines can.

So far, so disgusting and we haven't even got to the slime yet. Oh yes, the slime. To escape predators, hagfish secrete a sticky goo that will allow them a slippery exit. They can produce gallons of the stuff in mere minutes, from hundreds of pores that line their body. Anything that dares attack them soon has a face full of this gill-clogging slimy secretion, and has to abandon the assault. It is a disgusting defence that saves the hagfish from all sorts of predators including wreckfish, conga eels and even sharks. To prevent choking on their own slime, they tie themselves in knots, which travel down the length of their body, scraping off excess mucus. They have even evolved the ability to sneeze to free their gills from the gloop. Canadian researchers are developing practical uses for the slime. They hope that it might make a great fabric for the catwalk: when the slime dries out, it becomes a silky, stretchy substance.

There are about 100 species of hagfish; one is critically endangered, two are endangered, six are vulnerable to extinction and two are near threatened.

HAGFISH

(*Myxini*)

'... performs its *amazing acrobatic feats* while carrying a heavy load on its back.'

THE WORD 'SLUGGISH' means 'slow, inactive, inert or lethargic', and so the last thing that one might expect from a slug is acrobatics. Yet the dromedary jumping-slug is an athlete worthy of being entered into the animal Olympics. Furthermore, it does indeed live on the Olympic Peninsula of Washington as well as some other areas of western North America, including British Columbia, Canada. It is threatened by the incursion of logging and transport infrastructure, causing the fragmentation of its habitat. This limits its ability to disperse and makes it easier for predators to reach it. The species is endangered but the Canadian the authorities are taking active measures to protect its habitat. There are seven varieties of jumping slug in this region but the dromedary jumping-slug is the most energetic.

When attacked by a predator, this slug performs a vigorous evasive manoeuvre in the form of a flip that can launch it to safety. It does this by contorting the body quickly in a corkscrew pattern so it is no longer adhering to the ground and tumbles to freedom. This convolution also dissociates it from its slime trail, meaning that certain predators find it harder to track. Not only is it capable of dexterous twists and turns; it performs its amazing acrobatic feats while carrying a heavy load on its back. It is named the dromedary jumping-slug after the one-humped camel, the dromedary. The slug bears a knapsack-like lump on its back, where it keeps its internal organs wrapped up in a small internal shell. The shell is partially visible as it pokes out a little through a nick in the skin.

These slugs can grow to be between 3 and 6cm and breathe using a primitive lung that is a cavity within the mantle and has a single opening on the right side of the body.

Like most gastropods, the group of molluscs that contains all slugs and snails, the dromedary jumping-slug is a hermaphrodite, meaning that it possesses both male and female reproductive organs. An individual typically lays clutches of fifty or so grey, jelly-like eggs on damp, decaying logs. It comes out mostly at night, finding its way around using powerful olfactory organs kept at the ends of the four tentacles on its face. It is thought to be herbivorous and probably feeds on fungi, moss and lichens, using a file-like ribbon, called a radula, to grate its food into manageable pieces.

DROMEDARY
JUMPING-SLUG

(*Hemphillia dromedarius*)

YOU MAY HAVE noticed that many of the bizarre creatures featured in this book are deemed ugly because of the king-size nature of their noses; this animal has quite the opposite problem.

The Tonkin snub-nosed monkey is one of the most endangered primates in the world and the largest primate species of Vietnam. It was presumed extinct for a long time before its joyous rediscovery in 1989, and has been classed as critically endangered since then. It is one of five members of the Rhinopithecus genus, all of which are endangered and have similarly underdeveloped noses. All of the other types of snub-nosed monkeys were thought to live in China, but a new species has recently been discovered in Myanmar, the state formerly known as Burma. It is said that when it rains, the water can gather on the top lip of the Myanmar snub-nosed monkey, tickling its naked nostrils and causing it to sneeze.

With its unusual and distinctive broad and pancake-flat face, its flat, upturned nose, white, tufted ears, baby-blue rings around the eyes, and thick, rubbery, pink lips, the Tonkin snub-nosed monkey is the most flamboyant looking of the group. It has an almost comical appearance, looking like a spoilt child that has raided its mother's make-up kit or a stuck-up, yet despondent, clown.

It inhabits the subtropical primary evergreen forest of the karst limestone hills and mountains. It clambers through the canopy, feeding on leaves, fruits, flowers and seeds. It mostly roams on all fours, leaping from tree to tree and hanging from branches with the help of a prehensile tail, rarely coming to ground. Groups generally consist of one adult male and a clique of fourteen or so females. Groups often cluster together at night, enjoying the comparative safety that comes in numbers.

The main threat to this pastel-painted primate is deforestation. So much of its habitat has been destroyed that it is now restricted to just five areas. Furthermore, though hunting has been banned and they apparently taste awful, some people still shoot them on sight. The population has recently been estimated to be only about 250 individuals but, fortunately, efforts to protect them and conserve areas of their habitat seem to be helping and their numbers in the wild are on the increase. Such news gives us hope for the species and shows how government support and working with local communities can make conservation efforts pay off.

'... like a *spoilt child* that has raided its mother's make-up kit ... or a *despondent clown*.'

TONKIN
SNUB-NOSED MONKEY

(*Rhinopithecus avunculus*)

SOUTHERN GROUND-HORNBILL

(Bucorvus leadbeateri)

THE SOUTHERN GROUND-HORN-BILL is the largest hornbill in the world and perhaps this is what makes it reluctant to fly; it prefers to waddle around while looking for food rather than trying to force its great weight into the air. It can be over 1m in height and can weigh over 6kg, with males being considerably larger than females. Its plumage is mostly black, the exception being the white wing tips that are only visible when it does take flight.

The face and throat of the male is covered with patches of flesh the colour of a bruised tomato. The face of a female is much the same, but she has an island of almost violet flesh among the sea of red. Hornbills are known for their large and robust curved beak and the casque that sits on top of it. The casque of the southern ground-hornbill is only small when compared to the massive horns of some of its relatives. The purpose of the casque is not known for certain, but there is a great deal of speculation regarding its possible function. Many think that it may be involved in helping members of the same species recognise each other, or that it may play a role in sexual selection, as the casques of males are generally bigger than those of females. A clue may lie in the fact that the casques of many hornbill species are hollow, leading some biologists to suggest that they may help amplify the loud booming calls that those species make.

Southern ground-hornbill groups form a very vocal choir. A chorus of calls can usually be heard at distances of up to 3km, allowing a group to announce its presence and stake a claim to a large territory. They feed and breed in groups. They forage on the ground, seeking out a wide range of prey including insects, reptiles and small mammals, but will also eat seeds and berries and have even been observed picking parasites off warthogs. The hornbills live only in parklands from Kenya all the way south to South Africa; their range is limited by a lack of suitable trees in which to build nests.

It is a co-operative breeder and each baby is usually cared for by its parents and at least two other birds. Not only does this help rear a chick, but it gives juvenile birds essential experience that they need in order to rear young themselves when they grow up. In spite of such intensive care, each nest tends to manage to rear only one chick, even if a few eggs are laid. This might be partly down to the selfish first-born chick bullying and stealing food from its siblings. In some areas, conservationists collect the hatchlings left to starve and raise them by hand, hoping to reintroduce them into the wild. Being such a slow breeder and having much of its habitat under threat has made this species vulnerable.

'... patches of flesh the colour of a bruised tomato.'

WHEN YOU LOOK at a sawfish, you assume that it must have a penchant for DIY. Perhaps, if it were to team up with a hammerhead shark, it could set up a terrific underwater woodwork company. In fact, sawfish are also known as 'carpenter sharks', a misleading name because, although they are from the elasmobranch group along with their cousins the sharks, sawfish are actually more closely related to rays and skates. To make matters still more bewildering, there are several species known as saw sharks that, though similarly tooled up with a saw-shaped snout, belong to a relatively distant order on the elasmobranch family tree. And the taxonomic chaos doesn't end there, as there are about six members of the Pristus genus of sawfish, at least three of which are confusingly commonly known as largetooth sawfish. The confusion continues into a genetic level as it is likely several of these species can interbreed, hybridising as though to spitefully make life still harder for the biologists who study them. This sort of blending of organisms is known as a 'species complex', and complex seems an apt description, though the word 'mess' might be more appropriate. The entire genus might even just be variations of the same species. In any case, all the members of this haphazard family are either endangered or critically endangered. Their populations have declined to less than 10 per cent of historical levels, the result of habitat destruction and overfishing.

'... you assume that it must have a penchant for DIY.'

The long, tapered snout of the largetooth sawfish can be up to a fifth of the length of the body. The sawfish uses this weapon to root around in the mud at the bottom of lakes or estuaries or in the coastal shallows, seeking out prey, using electro-sensory cells that line the saw. Along the edge of the blade is a series of sixteen to twenty evenly spaced long, thin teeth. When lunch is located, the sawfish whips its head through the water, stunning, slashing or impaling its victim on the sharp spikes. The teeth are actually modified denticles, tiny teeth that cover its skin, giving it a sandpaper-like texture. In fact, in some parts of the world, the skin of sharks has been used as a sandpaper substitute, meaning that a part of the sawfish really is used in woodwork.

The largetooth sawfish can reach a length of up to 6.5m, weighing nearly 600kg. They would be much heavier but, like all elasmobranches, their skeleton is made from light and limber cartilage instead of hard and heavy bone. They are ovoviviparous, meaning that the young develop in an egg with a thin shell that the mother retains inside her body before they eventually emerge from the mother, fully formed. About eight pups are born at a time, all of them bearing a rubbery scabbard around their rostrum to protect their mother from harm while she gives birth. This sheath then falls away.

LARGETOOTH SAWFISH

(Pristis pristis)

W

HEN TIMES ARE hard, we should all think of the tenacious can-do attitude of dung beetles. When life seems poo, you just gotta roll with it!

'When life seems poo, you just gotta roll with it!'

Dung beetles are members of the Scarabaeoidea superfamily and are commonly known as scarabs. There are many thousands of varieties living across the globe. Most of them feed exclusively on dung and employ three main tactics to do this. 'Tunnellers' bury dung where they find it, while 'dwellers' live in it permanently, only leaving to find a fresh pile in which to breed. The most famous type of dung beetles are the 'rollers' who prefer to make their meals into takeaways, fashioning dung into spheres and rolling it away to bury it elsewhere. They feed on these balls and males also use them to entice mates. If a female spots a male with a ball of manure she fancies, she will join him on his journey and together they will roll it to an area of soft soil where they can bury the ball. They will mine their way into the ball and build a brooding chamber from a mix of dung and saliva, laying a single egg at the heart of each ball.

To do this, they have to be real body-builders and are among the strongest insects on the planet, being able to lift over 1,000 times their own weight. It is no wonder that they have long been revered. The ancient Egyptians believed that the sun was a massive fiery dung ball, rolled across the sky by a celestial scarab.

While most species of dung beetle are surviving quite well, there are a few that are endangered, including the flightless dung beetle of South Africa. Its numbers are dwindling as a by-product of the declining numbers of elephants and other large herbivores. Furthermore, as a flightless creature that is hard to spot, it is frequently run over on the roads, a threat which has prompted one South African safari park to put up 'dung beetle crossing' signs.

Like many dung beetles, the South African flightless dung beetle can only roll its ball by going backwards and in a straight line. It struggles to deal with the intense heat of the overhead sun and so moves at a pace that allows its feet to touch the ground only briefly. It frequently stops to climb atop the moist ball of faeces or lick its feet to keep them cool.

Some beetles evade the burning heat by gathering their dung only at night. These beetles, like sailors of old, navigate using the heavens and are currently the only insects known to orient themselves using the Milky Way. They may well be stuck in the dirt, but they are looking at the stars.

'... they have to be real body-builders ...'

FLIGHTLESS
DUNG BEETLE

(Circellium bacchus)

GHOST BAT

(Macroderma gigas)

THE LOOKS OF many of the species in this book are considered unpleasant on account of the excessive size of their nose or ears. Well, this species must be perhaps three times as horrid then, having both super-size and strangely shaped nose and ears. Looking like an extra from a horror film, the ghost bat is so named for the spectrally pale colour of its long, soft fur and naked, fleshy wings. With a 60cm wingspan, it can seem quite spooky while flying at night. It looks as if it is wearing a size twelve skin on a size ten body. This is important for flight; the membrane links the digits of the forelimbs together into vast webbed wings, making bats the only mammals naturally capable of true and sustained flight.

The other common name of the species is no more comforting – the false vampire bat. It was once thought that it was a bloodsucker, like a true vampire bat. It is, however, a voracious hunter and one of the most carnivorous of all bats. As darkness falls, it emerges from its roost in a cave or rocky outcrop, commuting to a favoured patch, where it lies in wait. It preys on large insects, small mammals, lizards, frogs, birds, and even other bats. When a victim approaches, it drops from above in a devastating ambush, killing it with a fearsome bite to the head or neck. It then hauls the corpse back to its perch or roost to enjoy it.

It has a nose worthy of Nosferatu. It is covered with a fleshy cartilage-reinforced protuberance known as a nose leaf. Bats use these curved, satellite dish-shaped patches of skin to focus the ultra-sound calls they make during echolocation. They broadcast sound waves in high-pitched squeaks and then, using their enormous ears, listen out for the echoes bouncing back from nearby surfaces to try to build an audio picture of their surroundings.

The ghost bat typically roosts alone, but in the breeding season females club together during pregnancy to form maternity colonies. Only ten such sites are known. A mother generally gives birth to a single offspring each year and carries it with her for the first four weeks, after which it is left at home in the roost and prey brought back to it until it is fully independent after about three months.

The ghost bat lives across a variety of habitats in northern Australia. Its range was once much larger: its disappearance from southern and central Australia may be partly due to natural increases in aridity in these areas. Many of its roost sites are being disturbed by mining, quarrying and even tourism. The bat is quite paranoid and will leave a roost if people enter. It is also having to compete for food with introduced species like cats and foxes, and so is considered vulnerable.

'... a nose worthy of *Nosferatu.*'

PERHAPS IT WENT bald with the worry about its potential demise; it was on the brink, after all. By the end of the 1980s there were only eight California condors left in the wild. Their numbers had been drastically reduced at first due to the decline in large native mammals. They took a second hit later thanks to humans shooting them, collecting their eggs and indirectly poisoning them with lead as the condor scavenged from carcasses contaminated with lead shot. Seeing how close the species was to annihilation, conservationists captured those last eight survivors to allow them to breed in safety. They would trick female birds into laying twice as many eggs by taking her clutch and putting them into an incubator, prompting the mother to lay a second batch. They even raised orphan chicks using hand puppets. The good news is that the bizarre bird pantomime worked and since 1992 many condors raised in captivity have been released back into the wild. It has been slow progress, but the conservation efforts are paying dividends and the first wild condor chick for over two decades was born in 2002.

The California condor is the largest bird in America, having a massive wingspan of nearly 3m. It soars, rising on thermal air currents to dizzying heights, up to 4,600m from the ground, scanning far below for anything big and dead to feast upon. When it finds something, it will gorge itself and has to stay on the ground for quite a while, nursing its full belly.

Its head is a rough, reddish colour surrounded by a rich black ruff. Its plumage is jet black but with contrasting white patches under each wing. The neck has an inflatable pouch, which it blows up like an erotic whoopee cushion to impress mates. They usually pair for life and raise a single chick together about every other year.

There are only two species of condors: the California condor and the Andean condor of South America. They are New World vultures and, in spite of the name, are not closely related to the Old World vultures of Africa and Asia. They only look so similar because of convergent evolution; they look the same because they do the same sort of jobs in their ecosystem. It seems that being big, bald and ugly is the best way to be a scavenger if you are a bird, and so evolution has come up with the same hideous blueprints on different continents.

'... *the* **bizarre** *bird pantomime* ...'

CALIFORNIA CONDOR
(*Gymnogyps californianus*)

THE HUMPHEAD WRASSE gets its common name from the prominent bump on the top of its head. The bulge grows grander with age and the males sport particularly huge ones, which combine with their large lips to give them the appearance of a crooning teddy boy. It is a long-lived fish, with a possible lifespan of over 30 years. It can grow to be enormous, almost 2m long, and covered with a patterned skin that varies from electric blue to a dull green in males and a range of rusty oranges in females. It roams over steep-shelving coral reefs in search of hard-shelled prey such as molluscs, starfish, or crustaceans. It also tackles tougher food and is one of the few fish known to have a stomach sturdy enough to handle the poisonous crown-of-thorns starfish, the deadly box jellyfish and toxic sea hares. The crown-of-thorns starfish is a fierce carnivorous predator that munches on coral and studies have shown that an individual starfish can consume up to 6m^2 of coral per year, decimating entire reefs. The humphead wrasse is one of the few species that police the rampant spread of these coral-killers and so plays a very important role in its ecosystem.

I imagine it is secretly envious of its poisonous prey, as the wrasse has had the evolutionary misfortune of being quite tasty to the human palate, though you would have thought that one look at them might have been enough to turn a diner vegetarian. The fish has never been common, and it has been continually hunted as a highly prized treat. In recent years though, as levels of wealth have increased in many East Asian countries, more people have started to demand this luxury meal. It has become the most highly sought species of the live reef food fish trade. Its rarity has not brought it protection, but instead seems to have pushed the price up and up. Humphead wrasse can fetch up to US $100 per kilogram at retail in Hong Kong markets, and, as their numbers dwindle, the rarity of the species is likely to increase the price higher still, which in turn will give hunters and fishermen more of an incentive to persecute the big-headed fish.

Though the wrasse is immune to the deadly venoms of notorious creatures like the crown-of-thorns starfish, it is still vulnerable to other poisons. Cyanide is typically used to catch fish for this trade, incapacitating it so it can be taken alive and kept fresh. This poison kills many other species of nearby fish as a violent by-product. It is hoped that trade restrictions will help save this endangered species and the reef as a whole.

*'The **bulge** grows grander with age ...'*

HUMPHEAD WRASSE

(*Cheilinus undulatus*)

GIANT GIPPSLAND
EARTHWORM
(Megascolides australis)

YOU MIGHT WELL think that there is nothing more icky and disgusting than a worm. You are wrong; there is one thing – a GIANT worm.

The people of Mongolia tell tall tales of a bloodthirsty, saveloy-red worm that hides beneath the sands of the Gobi desert. It is said to be 1.5m long and as thick as a man's arm, with skin the colour and texture of the bloodied intestines of a cow. They say that it can kill; that touching it will cause it to spit an acrid acid or unleash a lethal electrical charge. These reports, as far as we can tell, are merely the stuff of legend. But there *are* giant worms out there, and much of their biology remains a mystery.

The giant Palouse earthworm of Washington, USA, is one of the largest earthworms in the world and, though there have been reports of it being able to grow up to 1m in length, the largest confirmed sightings have been but 30cm. At such a size it doesn't deserve the name 'giant', but 'slightly-bigger-than-average Palouse worm' doesn't quite have the same ring to it. They do not spit or release dangerous shocks like an electric eel, but they have been studied by using hi-tech probes that run an electric current through the soil, prompting the worms to come to the surface.

A close cousin of the giant Palouse earthworm is the Oregon giant earthworm, which is rumoured to grow to be up to 1m in length and to smell strangely like lilies when handled. The rumours cannot be confirmed though, as no one has seen one since 1981 and many fear that they could be extinct.

There is at least one species of earthworm which has had its colossal size confirmed. The Gippsland giant earthworm of Australia was first discovered in the 1870s and was first thought to have been, perhaps, some strange kind of snake. The worms average 1m in length, though individuals of 3m have been reported. They live in deep burrows and never come to the surface, unless flushed out and forced to flee by heavy rains.

*'... little is known about these **weird** worms ...'*

It may be that little is known about these weird worms because they live so much deeper in the soil than common garden varieties and we just don't have the chance to study them very often. However, it is more likely that the introduction of invasive species of non-native worm predators and the effects of the construction industry are killing them off. All these giant species are considered vulnerable, but many scientists suspect that their situation could be considerably worse than feared.

*'... their situation could be considerably **worse** than feared.'*

IT MAY LOOK like a particularly nosy hedgehog, but the long-beaked echidna is so much more. It is a rebel that doesn't do things the way other mammals do. All of its kin, the monotremes, seem peculiar to us. They form an ancient group that is one of the earliest branches of the mammal family tree, having diverged from all the other forms millions of years ago. Fossil evidence indicates that their body has changed very little over the last 100 million years. All of the surviving examples of monotremes, the echidnas and the platypus, are indigenous to Australia and Papua New Guinea, although there is evidence that they were once more widespread.

There are four different types of echidna. The most common is the short-beaked echidna, found throughout Australia, Tasmania and Papua New Guinea. The other three types only live on the islands of Papua New Guinea and are all on the verge of extinction. The smallest and rarest species is known from only one specimen found in 1961 and has been named Attenborough's long-beaked echidna, in honour of the famous wildlife broadcaster. Attempts to track it down have been fruitless, but local hunters have claimed to have spotted it very occasionally. The other two species are very similar and have only recently been declared as separate species when scientists noticed that the eastern long-beaked echidna has one more claw on its forelimbs than the western long-beaked echidna.

Monotremes are unusual in that, unlike all other mammals, they lay leathery eggs. In echidnas, breeding seems to be seasonal, with the female laying between four and six eggs in her pouch each July. Hatching occurs about ten days later, and the young echidnas, known rather cutely as puggles, remain in the pouch for a further six or seven weeks until the spines develop and the mother ejects her prickly little offspring from her pocket. By that stage, they probably make her itch. Monotremes do suckle their young but, rather than having nipples like all other mammals, they use specialised patches of skin, which sweat a nutritious milk.

'... young echidnas, known rather cutely as *puggles* ...'

The snout of the long-beaked echidna can be up to two-thirds of the length of the head. The narrow mouth has no room for teeth; instead it has evolved spikes that cover the tongue, which can act like Velcro to help it snatch prey and draw it into the mouth. It feeds almost exclusively on earthworms, but may occasionally nibble on termites and ants or use its powerful claws to rip open rotting wood in search of insect larvae. The skin on the snout of an echidna is dotted with electro-receptors that enable it to pick up the weak electrical fields given off by other animals. This helps the echidna to use its nose like a metal detector, swishing it around in an attempt to locate invertebrate prey in the dark. Similar electrosensory abilities are also present in the bill of its close cousin, the platypus.

EASTERN LONG-BEAKED ECHIDNA

(*Zaglossus bartoni*)

MYERS' SURINAM TOAD is both one of the most evolutionarily distinct and one of the most disgusting amphibians in the world. Even when at the peak of health, this toad from North America looks almost putrefied. But not only does it appear decayed: it looks as if it has lost a fight with a lorry. Its wart-encrusted body is so flattened that it seems as though it has been run over. As such, it is unable to adopt the well-known upright posture of a hopping frog and instead it spends all of its life underwater, swimming with its powerful hind legs and strangely lobed forelimbs splayed out to its sides.

It doesn't have any teeth or even a tongue (it doesn't even really have a neck), making it hard to distinguish where the carbuncle-covered body ends and the hideous head begins. The only thing that it seems to have going for it anatomically is an amazing pair of incredibly sensitive, lobed front limbs. It uses these dexterous digits, each forked into feeler-like tendrils, to detect its prey, mostly invertebrates, hiding in the mud. These fingers are even freakier when seen under a microscope, as they appear to subdivide into smaller ends for heightened sensitivity. It is because of these jazz-hand appendages that members of the Pipa genus are frequently known as star-fingered toads. Once found, prey is quickly forced into the great gummy gape of the toad's mouth.

Stranger still is its bizarre, elaborate and athletic mating behaviour. First, the male engages the female in a coital cuddle that can last for over a day. During this embrace, the female's back swells, becoming engorged with blood. Then, like a pair of squashed gymnasts, they start to somersault in synchrony. The male massages the female and, while upside down, she expels her eggs on to his abdomen before they flip over once more so that the eggs adhere to her sticky swollen back and here, mid-tumble, he fertilises them. Each rotation takes about twelve seconds and the pair repeat their raunchy rough and tumble routine approximately fifteen times, releasing about 100 eggs in total. The male will sometimes use his feet to help spread the eggs over the female's back, like a layer of spawn jam. The eggs slowly develop, gradually sinking into the skin of the female, and she will carry them with her everywhere she goes until, weeks later, an infestation of tadpoles hatches and emerges, bursting from her flesh. In related species of the Pipa genus, the babies can hatch out as fully formed froglets.

The species is endangered because of water pollution and the destruction of the forests surrounding the wetlands that are its home.

'... hard to distinguish where the **carbuncle-covered** body ends and the hideous head begins. '

MYERS' SURINAM TOAD

(*Pipa myersi*)

THE JUVENILE BUMPHEAD parrotfish is a mottled, pretty little fish covered in cute white spots. It is a shame it grows up to look as though it has had a frightful knock to the noggin.

The bumphead parrotfish, also known as the green humphead parrotfish, is the largest of the parrotfish, a group that gets its name from their peculiar teeth, which are fused into a parrot-like beak. They use this beak to scrape algae and live corals into their mouth and have a further set of teeth at the back of the throat which grind up their food to aid swallowing. The bumphead parrotfish uses its bulging forehead as a battering ram, bashing into the coral to break it down into smaller, more digestible pieces. Any hard, non-nutritious material is passed out in the fish's faeces and goes on to make sediment that plays an important role in the reef ecosystem, contributing to the make-up of the shoreline. Adult bumphead parrotfish are estimated to consume 5 to 6 tonnes of coral each year, meaning that a large number of beach paradises in Australia and the Pacific Rim are made mostly of parrotfish poo.

Bumpheads are sociable creatures and usually travel in small shoals. They can grow to be 130cm and live to be up to 40 years old. Groups often congregate together at night to sleep in tightly knit crowds. Some species of parrotfish coat themselves in a membrane of mucus, which they spit from their mouths and inflate, outside the body, by breathing out through their gills. This snot sleeping bag is thought to afford them some protection while they nap, by clogging the mouth of would-be predators, and helping the fish notice nearby movements and make a head start on escape. The skin itself is coated in another mucous substance that may repel parasites and act as a natural sun cream to prevent the fish being burnt by the powerful tropical sun.

Once a month, under the romantic light of the full moon, they gather in large groups of over 100 individuals to spawn. It is their gregarious nature that has led the species to become vulnerable to extinction: spear fishermen find it easy to locate the large groups. They have been hunted relentlessly and this once abundant fish is now virtually extinct in Guam, the Marshall Islands, parts of Fiji and East Africa. Conservationists are seeking to create safe havens where the parrotfish can spawn in peace.

'... a large number of **beach paradises** in Australia ... are made mostly of parrotfish poo.'

BUMPHEAD PARROTFISH

(Bolbometopon muricatum)

BLUE-GRAY
TAIL-DROPPER SLUG
(Prophysaon coeruleum)

I**N NORTH AMERICA** there is a group of slimy slugs that have a particularly strange secret. They live in moist conditions, feeding in the undergrowth and leaf litter and, if you scare them, their bum drops off!

'... their *bum* drops off!'

Leaving behind your tail might well seem like the ultimate act of carelessness but it is far from it. Any predator grabbing hold of the tail is suddenly no longer holding the whole slug, allowing the remaining part of the body to scarper with its vital organs intact. Or it could be that the tail is left behind as a bribe, a readymade meal that draws the attention of a hungry predator, and allows the slug to leg it, or at least, leg it as much as something with no legs can.

The proper biological name for this dramatic escape technique is autotomy, coming from the Greek meaning 'self-severing', and is a tactic employed by a wide variety of taxa. There are molluscs, spiders, crustaceans, insects, geckoes, skinks, lizards, amphibians and even mammals which all seem to perform some form of DIY amputation in response to an attack. In most cases, the decision to ditch a limb comes about only when the animal is grasped by a predator and means that the escapee is granted a quick getaway with a lightened load and nothing holding it back. Some spiders lose a limb in response to a venomous sting or bite and so prevent the damaging toxin from spreading through the body to do more widespread harm. In the case of some bees, the barbed sting can become lodged in the skin of its enemy and, when the bee flies off, it leaves this anchor, which acts like a rip cord and tears the rest of the bee's abdomen apart. The bee dies but it is a clever kamikaze act of war. The explosion of the abdomen releases a wave of pheromones that act like a flare, warning other members of the hive of nearby danger and pinpointing where the enemy is. There are many insects where the male leaves his reproductive organs lodged within the female to get on with mating in his absence. In many cases the male dies; in others it simply goes off to do other things, making this an extreme example of multi-tasking.

In many of these cases of self-sacrifice, the animal is able at least partially to regrow its missing appendages and scientists are studying these species in the hope of developing techniques that will one day allow us to regrow damaged organs and repair our body without the need for surgery. Many of the genes used for successful seamless regeneration are common to both these species and to us humans, but are regulated and switched off in our adult bodies.

Perhaps the most striking and strange species of tail-dropper slug is the Canadian blue-grey variety, which is the bright blue colour of a slimy Smurf. It is endangered and known from only five locations on southern Vancouver Island. Major threats to its existence include habitat loss and fragmentation due to land-clearing, heavy recreational use of habitat, and introduced species, including other slugs and snails.

CUBAN SOLENODON

(Solenodon cubanus)

IT MAY LOOK like a big and bumbling scruffy rat, but the Cuban solenodon carries a secret weapon. It is armed with nasty teeth and a potent venom cocktail in its saliva that it uses to disable its prey.

There are very few mammals that are venomous. There are a few types of shrew that have venomous spit, which scientists are studying, hoping to develop drugs from them to fight neuromuscular diseases, high blood pressure and some forms of cancer. It is thought that some moles may have similar venoms. Then there is the platypus, the male of which has strong spurs on his hind legs, hooked up to venom glands. Even some primates seem to be venomous. Some species of slow loris produce venom from their brachial glands – specialised sweat glands by their elbows. They can lick these patches, transferring the venom to their tooth comb, a special set of incisors primarily used for grooming, and then pass it on through a bite. The venom is mild and only seems toxic to certain susceptible species. And then there are the highly unusual and truly venomous solenodons.

The Cuban solenodon is one of only two remaining species in its genus and the family Solenodontidae, meaning 'slot-toothed ones'. They use the grooves in these teeth to inject their toxic saliva directly into a victim's blood stream, in a manner very similar to that of a snake. Their family is ancient, having branched off from the other mammals some 75 million years ago. This suggests that venomous mammals were probably much more common millions of years ago.

They are nocturnal, and spend most of the day hiding in rock clefts, hollow trees or burrows. At night they search for food, using their long snout to root around for insects and spiders, and their claws to uncover or dig them up.

The Cuban solenodon is perhaps the scraggier of the pair, the Hispaniolan variety somehow managing to make the long shrew-like nose and rough coat seem almost cute. Though they are currently classified in the same genus, genetic studies suggest that they are quite distant cousins. Their lineages diverged some 25 million years ago when the islands on which they live moved apart geologically. They show degrees of genetic distinctiveness, leading some biologists to argue that they should perhaps not only be recognised as separate species but be recategorised in separate genera. Recently, the populations of Hispaniolan solenodon that live in the Dominican Republic and Haiti have become viewed as a separate subspecies.

Both species of solenodon are endangered as they have a limited capacity to reproduce, taking years to reach sexual maturity and only having one or two offspring a year. Most of their preferred forest habitat has now been lost to agriculture and development, and only an estimated 15 per cent of the island's original vegetation cover remains. They are slow, clumsy movers and, though they are armed with chemical weaponry, they have simply not evolved to be able to cope with the predators that European settlers brought with them and make easy targets for dogs, cats and mongooses.

'... armed with chemical weaponry ...'

PART SALAMANDER, PART sausage, this frankfurter-like amphibian is known as an olm. It lives in the cavernous pits below the ground of Slovenia, Croatia, and Bosnia and Hertzegovina, making it the only vertebrate in Europe that is adapted to spending all of its life in caves.

The olm is a member of the Proteidae, an ancient family of salamanders that consists of only six species and generally known as mudpuppies and waterdogs. Their lineage diverged from their closest relatives some 190 million years ago. While most salamander life cycles go through an aquatic larval period before metamorphosing into adults, all members of the Proteidae petulantly refuse to grow up: they retain their gills, which look like flamboyant, pink feather boas, throughout their lives. The olm's eyes are laughable and most don't even bother growing eyelids: in fact, one subspecies even wears a permanent layer of skin over them. In the larval form their eyes are normal, but then, as though the olm suddenly remembers that it lives in total darkness, the eyes diminish and start to regress, disappearing almost totally after about four months. Being unable to see and living in an environment where sight is useless, they rely on other senses: the best sense of smell of any amphibian; hearing adapted and specialised to work underwater; a compass-like awareness of magnetic fields to help navigate in the inky blackness of their home; and the ability to detect weak electric fields, allowing them to feel the presence of a nearby prey's nervous system. Armed with these senses, the olm hunts and feeds upon crabs, snails, insects and other small cave invertebrates. If food is scarce, though, they can survive without eating for up to ten years. They do this by sheer laziness, lowering their metabolism and, when particularly desperate, can even reabsorb their own body tissues. They are a long-lived species and, in captivity, have been observed living to over 58 years old, though some evidence suggests that they can survive for up to 100 years. In most cases, their skin has a pasty white or pinkish hue and, as they are mostly transparent, the sexes can be easily distinguished by examining their brashly displayed internal organs. In 1986 a dark-skinned subspecies, known as the black olm, sporting normal eyes, was discovered in Slovenia and scientists now believe that the olm might be a complex of several subspecies.

The olm is considered vulnerable. Its numbers are declining due to over-collection from the wild, the introduction of invasive species and from the pollution of the waters in which it lives.

'Part salamander, part sausage ...'

OLM

(Proteus anguinus)

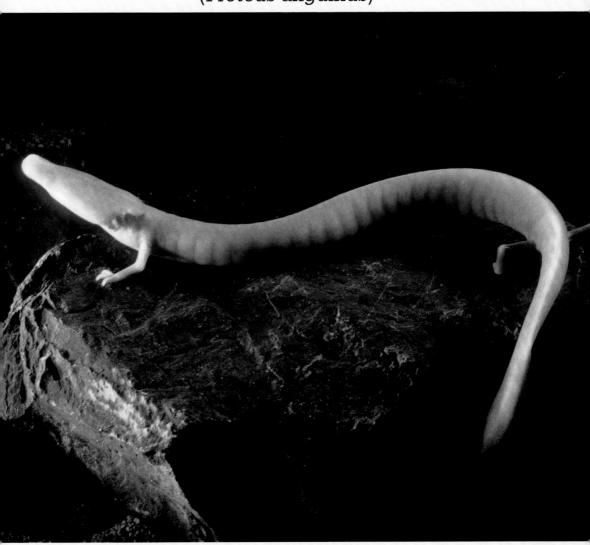

IT MUST REALLY suck to be a razorback sucker. The fish was once widely distributed through the Colorado River and the calm, flat waters of its major tributaries, but since the development of the dams, the introduction of other fish for sport and the large-scale use of water for industry and domestic purposes, it has become critically endangered. No wonder it has a chip on its shoulder.

Razorbacks, also known as humpbacks, are the largest species of suckers that live in the Colorado River and reach a maximum length of 90cm. They are a long-lived species; older fishes have been estimated at more than 40 years, with both males and females reaching maturity at the age of 4. The razorback spends most of its life in the deeper portions of the river, feeding on algae, insect larvae and plankton. To breed, it has to move to the shallower areas, where males do their best to stake out breeding territories. The eyes of the razorback are adapted to be receptive to parts of the ultraviolet spectrum; this at first seems unusual, as UV rays cannot pass through water to the depths at which the sucker normally lives. However, its eyes have another adaptation, in the form of a highly reflective iris. This means that when a male notices a rival male entering its breeding territory, it can roll its eyes, as if in an expression of exasperation, and flash its competitor a signal in ultraviolet light.

'... it can roll its eyes, as if in an expression of **exasperation** *...'*

This acts like hazard lights on a car, warning rival males not to come any closer. What is particularly clever about this adaptation is that, as UV light does not travel well underwater, this signal can be seen close up as a garish warning to other males, but is not so brash and bright that it gives away the razorback's location to any carnivorous fish out on the hunt. Females do not react to the eye flashes at all.

Spawning occurs in late winter or spring, when females are attended by groups of up to a dozen males. They settle on the riverbed together and release their gametes en masse, the female spawning several times with many males. The adhesive eggs stick to the gravel on the riverbed and stay there until they hatch. Though many millions of eggs may be laid, only a tiny percentage of them will survive and they are particularly vulnerable to cold weather. Furthermore, many introduced species of fish love to eat the eggs, and many might be lost as other forms of sucker hybridise with them to produce offspring that are less genetically razorback and less likely to survive.

*'Though many **millions** of eggs may be laid, only a tiny percentage of them will survive ...'*

RAZORBACK SUCKER

(*Xyrauchen texanus*)

LORD HOWE ISLAND
STICK INSECT

(Dryococelus australis)

'... the large, flightless Lord Howe Island stick insect was eaten into **presumed extinction** *within two years.'*

THE LORD HOWE Island stick insect does not, as its name would suggest, live on Lord Howe Island, Australia. No, it died out there. The island is a tiny volcanic dot about two hours' flight east of Brisbane and has no mobile phone reception, only 10km of road and only one policeman. Unfortunately though, it does have rats. Man first set foot in this paradise in 1788 and managed to keep from utterly decimating much of the indigenous wildlife until 1918, when we unwittingly introduced rats to the island and they started munching their way through any unique and wonderful species they could find. Many species, that until this point had never encountered such a deadly foe, went under and the large, flightless Lord Howe Island stick insect was eaten into presumed extinction within two years.

Fortunately, a tiny new population of only about thirty individuals was discovered on a tall and treeless volcanic rock, 23km east of Lord Howe Island. All the free-living members of the species live there within about 180m^2, surviving on only a single species of plant, and are viewed as critically endangered. It could take only a single freak weather occurrence to wipe them out.

To try to save the insect, access to their last wild range is tightly controlled and conservationists have been breeding them in captivity with remarkable success, with thousands of individuals currently living in zoos around the globe. It is hoped that, when rats are eventually eradicated from its ancestral home, the Lord Howe Island insect can be reintroduced.

It has a handy reproductive trick that has, perhaps, aided its survival. As well as reproducing by sexual reproduction, females can also have offspring independently, by a process known as parthenogenesis, whereby unfertilised eggs can develop into females, which are genetically very similar to their mother. She lays batches of about ten eggs at a time in holes dug in the soil and can produce up to 300 eggs in her lifetime. If a male is on the scene, a female and he may pair up and mate for up to 20 minutes, three or four times a night.

The babies, known as nymphs, hatch out a bright, vivid green colour and, over a series of moults, grow bigger and darker until they are over 10cm long and a glossy black colour. Their robust and spiky body has given them the nickname of 'land lobster'.

'Their robust and spiky body has given them the nickname of **"land lobster".'**

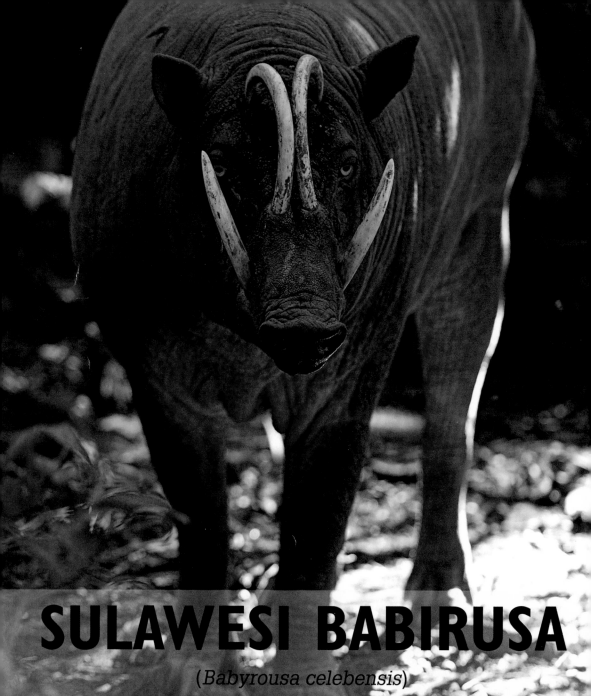

SULAWESI BABIRUSA
(Babyrousa celebensis)

IF THERE WAS ever a species of ugly, endangered animal that seemed to be doing its best to drive itself headfirst into extinction, it is surely the babirusa. You would swear that its bizarre tusks were specifically made for suicide.

'... doing its best
to drive itself headfirst
into **extinction** ...'

The male has its two enlarged lower canines poking out of its mouth to form tusks. This is not an unusual feature in pigs and their relatives; it is the other pair of tusks that is unique. The upper canines grow in the wrong direction entirely, growing upwards through the skull to emerge through the skin on the other side. What is stranger still is that these canines have a curve that sends them in a large ornate arc back down right between the eyes where they can start pushing back through the skull. It is no wonder that peoples of the island of Silawesi, Indonesia, where this weird hog is found, make demonic masks that mimic its face. They know it as the 'pig deer', as its tusks resemble a deer's antlers. Their function remains unclear, as their peculiar position means that they cannot be used for foraging and the upper canines are too frag-

ile to be much use in a fight. When males do clash, they rear up on their hind legs, trying to box with their front feet, or slash their opponent with the lower canines, which they keep sharp by grinding them against trees. Females sensibly do not have tusks at all; their canines either grow in step with their other teeth or are entirely absent.

There are three species of babirusa, spread across the islands of Wallacea in Indonesia. They were thought, until 2002, to represent variations of the same species. The Sulawesi babirusa is the largest of the family, being able to reach weights of up to 100kg. It is also the baldest of the batch, having only a sparse smattering of hairs coating its rough, mud-coloured skin. It is omnivorous and eats a varied diet including roots, fruits, nuts and leaves and will even hunt small animals. One of its favourite hangouts on Sulawesi is around the volcanic island's hot springs, where it can lick salt-encrusted rocks for essential sodium and socialise with other individuals. It sometimes seems to create makeshift nests in which to sleep or shelter from the rain. To give birth, the female builds a more precise home, scratching a shallow hollow in the earth about 3m long and lined with leaves and branches. There she gives birth to a small litter of one or two piglets at a time; she only has two teats with which to feed them.

'You would swear its **bizarre** tusks
were specifically made for **suicide**.'

CHINESE GIANT SALAMANDER

(*Andrias davidianus*)

THE CHINESE GIANT salamander is capable of growing to be up to 1.8m in length, making it the largest amphibian in the world. Looking like a mouldy sack of warts, its blotchy green-brown skin is a field of wrinkles through which the creature absorbs most of its oxygen. Although it spends all its life in water, it lacks gills and only occasionally comes to the surface for a gulp of air and to make use of the terrible pair of substandard lungs that it bears. Its lidless eyes are tiny and sit atop a large, broad, flat head, granting the salamander only poor vision. As such, it relies heavily on its acute sense of smell and touch to find its prey. Its diet is varied and features a wide variety of prey including fish, worms, insect larvae, frogs and their tadpoles, crustaceans, molluscs, reptiles and small mammals and, should it get the chance, carrion, its own manky shed skin and eggs, and other smaller Chinese giant salamanders. Its mouth is filled with small but numerous teeth that line not only the jaw, but the roof of the mouth as well. The bite is ferocious and provides a strong grip on its prey. The lower jaw is depressed quickly and the mouth opened wide to an angle of up to 40°, in a feeding method known as 'asymmetrical buccal suction', allowing prey to be quickly hoovered up into the cavernous gaping gob.

'... like a mouldy sack of **warts** *...'*

Chinese giant salamanders are generally nocturnal and spend most of their days hiding in dark crevices. The males, known as 'den masters', spend much of their time aggressively guarding their underwater burrows, subterranean bachelor pads that they dig into the banks of a stream. Females enter the brooding chamber and lay a string of about 500 eggs before leaving to allow the male to fertilise them and then spend the next fifty days or so protecting them until they hatch.

Though the giant salamander is seriously threatened, its populations decimated by habitat destruction, pollution, and the folk medicine trade, its salvation could come, ironically, from one of the reasons for its mass destruction. Its flesh is considered a delicacy throughout Asia and so attempts are being made to farm them. They taste delicious apparently and, even alive, are thought to have a hint of a peppery odour. Perhaps stranger still are their spooky calls that are said to sound like the voice of a child.

'Its **flesh** *is considered a delicacy throughout Asia ...'*

THE FACE OF the blobfish is a picture of abject misery. But it does have a right to look so depressed. Deep-sea trawling in its home territory off the coast of Australia and Tasmania has made it endangered. It is not even that we want to feast upon this strange beast; fishermen only catch it by mistake and throw it, dead, back into the ocean. They may look like deep-sea blancmange but they don't taste like it.

'... deep-sea blancmange ...'

In its natural environment it doesn't look quite so hideous or out of place. Its jelly-on-a-plate appearance is a result of gelatinous flesh and pathetic muscle tone. It lives at a depth of between 600 and 1,200m, where the pressure is many times greater than at sea level. This is so deep that the gas bladders used by most fish to float don't work. Instead the blobfish uses a fatty substance that fills its body; this substance is slightly less dense than water and allows the blobfish to stay just about buoyant enough to remain passively above the sea floor without wasting much energy. It bobs along

placidly, lazily waiting for food to come within reach. It mostly eats gormless sea urchins, molluscs and crustaceans that are too dumb and slow to escape.

It is often said that we know more about the surface of the moon than we do about the deepest recesses of our planet. Because blobfish live so deep down in the ocean, very little is known about the biology and ecology of the species. This is a general problem we have with sea-dwelling species; they are incredibly hard to study and the conservation status of most sea-life is unknown. We only know what it eats by looking at the contents of its dissected stomach. Much of what we think about the blobfish has to be inferred by learning about its relatives, most of which live in shallow water and can be studied with comparative ease. The blobfish is a member of the sculpin family, also known as the bullheads or sea scorpions because of the many spines that some species bear. It is thought that there are about 300 different types of sculpin, many of which are endangered. They live in both fresh and saltwater habitats and tend to have wide, heavy heads with elongated, tapered bodies that make them look superficially like tadpoles, though many are adorned with spines and fan-like fins.

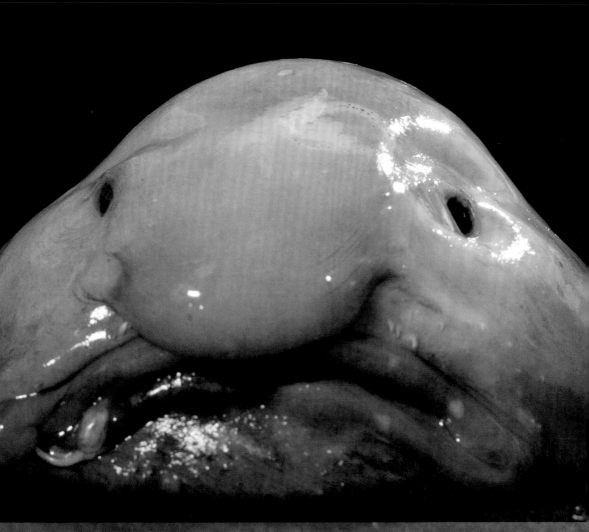

BLOBFISH

(*Psychrolutes marcidus*)

THIS UNUSUAL SPECIES of deer may look more like Dracula than Bambi, but its appearance is simply retro and tells us something about the ancestry of all deer. It is not from Transylvania, but is in fact a native of China and Korea. Approximately 10 per cent of its population is now based in England since a few individuals went AWOL from Whipsnade Zoo in 1929, and they have been thriving in the Fens and Broads of East Anglia. There is a feral population in France now as well, meaning that the survival of this vulnerable species looks more likely in spite of threats in China, where its population is shrinking. It is hunted for its meat and for use in traditional Chinese medicine and is suffering disturbance to its habitat.

The scientific name of the species translates loosely as 'unarmed water-drinker', referring to the Chinese water deer's lack of antlers and fondness for wetland habitats. One look at those fangs, though, makes you question the idea of them being unarmed. They hark back to the days before deer had evolved antlers to be used in their territorial and reproductive battles, and when most deer used tusks for fighting instead. The males live mostly solitary lives, staking out a territory using their urine and

piles of dung and marking trees by rubbing against them with specialised (and smelly) glands. They will defend their territory aggressively from rival stags. Males square up to each other, assessing their opponent through a ritualised parallel walk. They strut, side by side, and make loud clicking noises in an attempt to seem intimidating. If neither backs down, they lay into each other, slashing with their fangs.

The tusks are canines that can grow to be up to 8cm long in males and only about 0.5cm in females. The tusks may be worthy of a sabre-toothed tiger, but the water deer is a strict vegetarian. It can be quite picky and grazes selectively, nibbling the best bits from a range of plants, only turning to grasses and shrubs when times are hard. The fangs have a limited mobility and can be drawn back when eating.

Females form small peaceful groups and dominant males will mate with any females they can find in their territory. The males will make quiet wolf whistles to try to woo them. After a gestation period of about six months, females give birth to two or three offspring, an unusually high number for a deer. The fawns sport a brown coat dappled with white spots, which helps them blend in with dense vegetation.

'... the **fangs** ... can be drawn back when eating.'

CHINESE WATER DEER

(Hydropotes inermis)

'… this frog can teach us a little about geology and the *history* of our *planet.*'

IT'S FAT, IT'S purple, and it has a nose like a pig's. Maybe that's why this Indian frog spends almost all its life underground. But it shouldn't be so shy. The scientists who discovered it claimed it was a 'once in a century' find. In spite of looking like a second-hand fruit pastille, this frog can teach us a little about geology and the history of our planet.

The purple frog used to be considered the only surviving member of an ancient amphibian family called the Nasikabatrachidae, but in 2006 taxonomists merged this family into the Sooglossidae. Until around 120 million years ago, in the early Cretaceous period, India was joined to the eastern part of the ancient southern supercontinent Gondwana, which subsequently split apart into Australia, Antarctica, India, Madagascar and the Seychelles over millennia of movement of the earth's plates. This split was entirely down to the natural process of plate tectonics and nothing to do with artistic differences. As the continents fidgeted their way across the globe, they took the species that made their homes on them along for the ride; the closest relatives of the purple frog are four tiny frog species that were found in the Seychelles. It is thought that these two amphibian lineages diverged from a common ancestor that inhabited Gondwana prior to the break-up of this landmass, meaning that the purple frog is the sole survivor of a group of amphibians that evolved 130 million years ago.

For most of the year this burrow-dwelling frog lives underground, digging downwards, using its hind limbs like webbed spades. It hunts termites, ants and worms, using its sensitive snout to poke through its prey's network of underground tunnels. It then unleashes its quick-fire tongue to grasp prey small enough to fit through its narrow mouth.

The purple frog only comes to the surface for several weeks of the year to breed. The male uses a sticky skin secretion to glue himself into position atop the female in an erotic embrace. The eggs are fertilised and then the spawn is laid in shallow pools. They will hatch into tadpoles and later metamorphose into adult frogs.

Because the purple frog spends so much time underground, scientists struggle to study it. Only 135 purple frogs have been observed, with only three of these being female. Their population is thought to be in decline, thanks to the destruction of the forests for the cultivation of coffee and other crops, and so the species has been classified as endangered.

'… *fat* … *purple* … nose like a *pig*'s.'

PURPLE
PIG-NOSED FROG

(Nasikabatrachus sahyadrensis)

PACIFIC LAMPREY

(Lampetra tridentata)

WITH A BODY shaped like a pipe and a face full of teeth that makes it look like an elongated orbital sander, the Pacific lamprey is a member of an ancient family that has been unchanged for millennia. They are believed to be the most basal of all vertebrates.

The nightmarish mouth does stand out from their otherwise dull and dreary body and so it is hardly surprising that taxonomists seem obsessed by them. They, along with their cousins the hagfish, belong to the superclass agnatha, meaning 'before jaws'. The now-defunct name of their group, the 'cyclostomes', means 'round mouthed', and in many species the biological name has been derived by counting the teeth, as is the case with the Pacific tridentata lamprey, which means 'the three-toothed lamprey'. Who would want to get close enough to count?

The common name, 'lamprey', translates loosely as 'stone licker' and they are so-named for their habit of sucking onto stones to stay still in the current as they rest. Some species use that sucking ability for the purpose of skulduggery too, latching onto prey to vampirically suck their victims' blood. They have been seen on all sorts of species, ranging from small fish to massive whales. Attacks on humans have also occurred, but only when an unfortunate lamprey is starved and desperate. In these leech-like species, it is only the adult form that is parasitic, while the larval form is a more passive filter feeder. Most species of lamprey don't even bother trying to feed when they reach adulthood, becoming entirely obsessed with sex, and living off the fat reserves they built

'... becoming entirely **obsessed** *with sex ...'*

up while young. In almost all forms, as soon as breeding is over, they die. All lampreys are anadromous, meaning that they swim up rivers from the sea to spawn in the fresh water.

The Pacific lamprey is a parasitic lamprey from the Pacific coasts of North America and Asia. They spend half of their ten-year lives as larvae, hunkered in silt beds, emerging at night to feed. Some scientists call them the earthworms of the river. When they are fully grown, they swim to the ocean to spend two years seeking fresh blood before returning to the streams to spawn. At every stage of their lifecycle, they act as an important food source for other species.

They may look terrifying but they are actually an easily-caught prey. They are terrible swimmers and have high calorie, fatty flesh that makes them a prized and easy catch for fish, birds and mammals, including seals, sea lions, and even people. Tribes of indigenous American peoples have hunted them for centuries. Unfortunately, the development of dams has prevented the Pacific lamprey from being able to reach its spawning grounds and the species is now endangered. As a valued food source for so many species, the knock-on effects for the entire ecosystem could be disastrous and its decline has been linked to the disappearance of many fish, such as salmon, from these rivers.

THE DRACULA ANT of Madagascar does not, as you might expect, suck vampirically on the blood of its prey. No, its means of nutrition is much more bizarre.

Ant colonies are often viewed as 'super organisms'. Though they are made up of millions of different individuals, they are divided into 'castes', each of which, like an organ, has a different role to play and is utterly dependent on the rest of the colony, in the same way that an organ relies on the rest of the body. A colony can almost be thought of as one being. The queen and the few winged males are the reproductive organs, the sterile sisterhood of workers is the means of acquiring food and the larvae, in this case, are like the digestive system.

The primordial look of this pale popcorn-yellow-coloured ant sheds light on the relatedness of ants to wasps. As such, this species is thought to represent a 'missing link' in ant evolution. Perhaps its most obvious wasp-like characteristic is the distinctive extended abdomen, which has a vicious sting at the end. The blind workers use these stings to paralyse their prey before carrying it back to their colony. There, they feed it to the large-mouthed larvae that quickly gobble it up. The workers get their food by scratching holes in the skin of their young and then sucking on the haemolymph that they produce. Haemolymph is the technical term for the blue-grey blood of insects and other arthropods. Some of the workers take their bellyful of blood to the immobile queen at the heart of the colony and vomit it up to feed her.

Scientists refer to this strange feeding behaviour as 'non-destructive' cannibalism, as the nibbling and sucking that workers do to larvae does not kill them. However, it must harm them, or at least hurt a little, as the scar-covered grubs have been observed trying to wriggle away and flee when hungry workers enter their chamber. This is a highly unusual means of nutrition; biting and bleeding your colony's young does not seem like a great technique for survival, but it works. There are many kinds of ant that also rely on their larvae to feed them, though no others go as far as partial cannibalism. The grubs are digestion machines, so in some species the adult workers will feed them and then feed themselves on the spew that the young regurgitate. It is as though the workers have outsourced the task of digestion to their more specialist young and this has made them free to evolve mouth parts more suitable for grasping and carrying, rather than munching food into digestible pieces.

The species is critically endangered. The precise threats facing the Dracula ant are yet to be uncovered but it is unlikely to have anything to do with garlic, or stakes through the heart. Its decline is probably in some way related to the destruction of its habitat as Madagascar's human population surges and more land is cultivated or developed for human use.

'... *biting* and *bleeding* your colony's young does not seem like a great technique for survival ...'

DRACULA ANT

(Adetomyrma venatrix)

'... pimply, pear-shaped
***punk** of a fish ...'*

THIS PIMPLY, PEAR-SHAPED punk of a fish likes nothing more than to strut around the estuary of the lower Derwent River in Tasmania. That is the only location where it is to be found, and it was once common there. It is now considered critically endangered and is, in fact, one of the most endangered marine fish in existence. The species underwent a catastrophic decline in the 1980s and no one is quite sure why, though many suspect that the introduction of the northern Pacific seastar played a role. These seastars are voracious predators of shellfish and it is thought that they may also eat the eggs of handfish or the sea squirts upon which the eggs are attached. For many fish, which produce millions of eggs, this might not be such a disastrous event, but the spotted handfish only lays between 80 and 250 eggs. The female lays the eggs around the base of sea squirts, sea grasses and sponges, which perhaps help provide some form of protection or cover. She then guards them for seven to eight weeks until they hatch out into fully formed juveniles. Conservationists are trying to breed them in captivity with the hope of reintroducing these fish into the wild and bolstering the population.

The main distinguishing feature of the spotted handfish, other than its Mohawk fins, spot-covered skin and mouth fixed in a sneer, is its large strong fins that function quite like hands. It uses these splayed-finger fins along with its sturdy pectoral fins to walk in a kind of slow, swaggering motion across the floor of the riverbed. Though it prefers to meander by this hand-walking type of movement, it can still swim, propelling itself by moving the tail back and forth.

Like all forms of anglerfish, handfish have a fleshy growth on the front of their head in the form of a modified dorsal ray. In the case of most anglerfish, these act as lures and in some cases even glow. They attract prey and position it in dangerous proximity to the tooth-filled mouth. In other cases, the glowing ray acts like a beacon to help draw potential mates toward them. In the case of handfish, these lures are barely grown and don't glow at all; they are no more than small, fleshy protuberances. This nub and the bumpy flesh which is covered in denticles – tooth scales – is responsible for their other, less flattering, common name; wart anglers.

*'... its **Mohawk** fins, spot-covered skin*
*and mouth fixed in a **sneer** ...'*

SPOTTED HANDFISH

(*Brachionichthys hirsutus*)

SAIGA ANTELOPE

(Saiga tatarica)

G

ARGANTUAN, FLESHY NOSES are far from cool. In fact, their purpose is probably the exact opposite. The hooter of the Saiga antelope has likely evolved to help heat the cold air before it enters the lungs in the winter and to help it to breathe unimpeded in the dusty summer months. The Saiga antelope originally inhabited a vast area of the Eurasian steppes, from the foothills of the Carpathian Mountains and Caucasus as far as Mongolia, but is now critically endangered and only has small, dwindling populations in Russia, Kazakhstan, Turkmenistan, Uzbekistan and Mongolia.

Its coat is a light tan colour in the summer months, helping it to blend in with the sand of the desert. In winter, the hair grows longer and thicker for added insulation and turns white to make its camouflage more suited to snow. This unusual species of ungulate is thought to represent a missing link between the antelopes and the goats.

They are nomadic and migrate in large groups, travelling over 100km a day, from their summer pastures in the grassland to winter territories in the desert areas. As the nights start to draw in, hormones begin to flush through the male's blood stream, triggering the start of the 'rut', their mating season. The big, droopy nose of the male swells to become

'... crying **treacle**.'

bigger still and the tufts of hair below his eyes become coated in a sticky secretion, making the antelope look as though it is crying treacle. Males gather groups of between thirty and fifty females into harems to breed and aggressively fend off rivals, using their short, ringed antlers as weapons. Not only can their violent territorial fights be lethal but, with their mind totally preoccupied with sex, the males barely feed, meaning that up to 90 per cent may drop dead from exhaustion before the breeding season is over. The male population is further threatened by poaching for their horns. This means that the groups are mostly female and that there is now a shortage of males for breeding, causing a further decrease in their numbers. Most countries where they live have made moves to ban hunting and have made the trade in their horns illegal, but an illicit underground trade still continues.

These antelopes feed on a variety of grasses and shrubs, but the quality of their foraging territories is also declining due to overgrazing by domestic livestock. On top of their man-made troubles, they have become afflicted by a potentially deadly lung infection.

'... totally **preoccupied** with sex ... up to 90 per cent may drop dead from **exhaustion** before the breeding season is over.'

WITH A FLAT body and shovel-shaped head, this unusual salamander might seem innocuous but it carries a secret weapon. This nasty little newt has a dangerous secret up its sleeve, or more accurately, on its sides: it hides its spines on the inside.

'... armed with a flank full of shivs ...'

When threatened, it will convulse, shoving the tips of its sharp and pointed ribs through the skin of its sides. Not only is it then armed with a flank full of shivs, but as the elongated ribs rip through the flesh, they pass through glands that paint them with a powerful poison. There are twelve of these conspicuously coloured glands dotted uniformly along its sides. Any predator that dares pick up this prickly little amphibian will get more than it bargained for; having poison injected directly into the soft tissues of the mouth is both very painful and harmful. To try to warn away adversaries, the newt adopts a rigid anti-predator posture, curling up its flattened body to expose the bright red undersides of its tail and feet, normally hidden for the sake of camouflage.

What is perhaps even more incredible than this method of protection is how the salamander is capable of recovering from cutting through its own sides. It is immune to its own poison and quickly recovers, somehow repairing the wounds without leaving a scar or suffering from infection. Such regenerative feats are common among the amphibians and scientists are studying them, hoping to uncover ways in which we can create medical techniques to emulate them and repair our own organs and bodies.

Little is known about this species, perhaps because it spends five months a year in hiding below the earth, hibernating to avoid the harshest periods of winter. Even when above ground, it seems to spend most of its time hiding in crevices and the undergrowth, feeding on earthworms, small molluscs and beetles. It is thought that there may be as few as 300 mature individuals of this species, living in the low hill forests of Zhejiang Province, China.

It is long-lived and slow breeding, perhaps living to be over 20 years old and only reaching sexual maturity after a decade. This may become its downfall. Not only is its forest habitat being smashed by urbanisation, road construction and agriculture, but also the small semi-permanent pools by which it lays its eggs are becoming seriously polluted. Because of these factors, its slow rate of maturity and its tiny population size, the Chinhai spiny newt is considered critically endangered. Conservationists are doing their best to cordon off protected areas and create artificial pools to aid its reproduction.

CHINHAI SPINY NEWT

(*Echinotriton chinhaiensis*)

BELUGA

(Huso huso)

STURGEONS ARE PERHAPS the most endangered group of fish in the world. There are about twenty-seven species in total, all of which seem to be suffering. The beluga, or European sturgeon, is the biggest of the group and one of the most endangered. Larger individuals can be over 5m in length, making it not only one of the largest of freshwater fish but one of the largest predatory fish and a rival to even the infamous and ferocious great white shark. Females are generally about twenty per cent bigger than males. They mostly feed on fish, but have been known to attack waterfowl and seal pups. It takes a long time to grow so big, and so this species only enters adulthood after about 20 years, sometimes living to be well over 100 years old.

'... they also sport a rather **dapper moustache** *made of four feathery tactile organs ...'*

Their skeleton is mostly made up of cartilage but, instead of scales, their body is covered in a suit of bony armour plating, known as scutes. Adding to their unique appearance, they also sport a rather dapper moustache made of four feathery tactile organs, known as barbels, which hang from their shovel-shaped face.

They drag these barbels along the river or seabed, using them to detect prey hiding in the gravel or sand, by tasting their environment. It is hard to see in the murky waters of estuaries and lakes and so they must rely on senses other than sight for hunting. When they find something, they gobble it up whole, with a gummy grin. They somehow manage to be deadly in spite of not having any teeth.

There are two main reasons for the family's decline. Many species are anadromous, living at sea but having to return to rivers to breed, and so are in trouble as their spawning grounds are degraded by industry or blocked by dams. The primary culprit for their demise, however, is hunting for their roe. The beluga sturgeon in particular is hunted for its eggs, which are eaten as caviar by people snob-nobbing at parties. This has made the beluga famous and threatened: it is listed in Guinness World Records as the world's most expensive fish. Its swim bladder was once commonly used to help clarify beers and wines, but fortunately brewers have turned to other means of removing yeast from their beer instead. Unfortunately, the trade in caviar continues apace, with much of it being illegal, and the rarity of the species only serves to push up the price tag. The salvation of the species might come from the lumpsucker fish, which produces more sustainably sourced but similar-tasting eggs. We must save the sturgeon, as surely death by posh people is one of the worst ways to go.

PRICKLY REDFISH

(*Thelenota ananas*)

THE PRICKLY REDFISH is not a fish. Nor is it, as you might think at first glance, a red rug. It is a sea cucumber, which is not actually a cucumber either, though, having said that, it does still sometimes feature in salads. Those prickly spines might act as a deterrent against most predators, but it doesn't stop humans from gathering them to eat. It is regarded as a delicacy throughout much of East Asia and it is its overexploitation as a culinary delight that has led it to become endangered. It seems that the rarer it becomes, the more demand for it increases and the more money that diving fishermen can get for it. It can grow to be up to 70cm long and has a recorded maximum weight of 6kg. In the wild, it can live for between 5 and 10 years.

The prickly redfish is an echinoderm, a relative of the starfish and the sea urchin. Its firm and rigid body is not quite cylindrical but is in fact flattened slightly on the underside, where it is covered with orange-coloured tube feet, with which it crawls across the seabed in search of food. It is mostly nocturnal and acts as the ocean's clean-up crew, feeding on the dead and decaying remains of seaweeds and other rotting matter. As such, the prickly redfish play an important ecological role within their habitat, recycling nutrients that help other reef species flourish. They are distributed mainly in shallow coral reef areas, preferring to feed in ranges covered in rubble or a layer of coral sand.

Their body is reinforced by an endoskeleton that lies just below the skin, forming a network of calcified structures joined by connective tissue. They lack a true brain and central nervous system and instead have a neural ring near the head. They absorb oxygen by pumping water in and out through their rear end to a branched lung-like organ, known as a respiratory tree. When spawning, prickly redfish gather together and rear up, before releasing eggs and sperm en masse into the water from small pores near the head end of the body.

The prickles of the prickly redfish are their main form of protection, but some closely-related species of sea cucumber have a stranger and much more gross means of defending themselves. If molested, they can partially turn themselves inside out, shooting their guts out of their behind at the aggressor in a sticky network of toxic tubes. When the danger has passed, they simply relax and, over a period of a few weeks, regrow their digestive system.

'... not a fish. Nor ... a **red rug**.'

'Some species perform nimble dances to seduce a mate. The hooded seal, however, *blows its nose*.'

WHEN YOU LOOK at a baby or female hooded seal, you could be forgiven for thinking that this creature is actually quite cute. Take one look at a pompous male doing its best to impress, and you will soon change your mind.

Sexual selection is responsible for many of the natural world's most beautiful sights. The males of many species of bird, for example, wear bright and attractive plumage, while serenading the female with a beautiful song. Many species of mammal, like deer, come armed with antlers and engage in deft gladiatorial bouts to chase off rivals and attract the ladies. Some species perform nimble dances to seduce a mate. The hooded seal, however, blows its nose.

The hooded seal is so named for the fleshy nasal appendage that droops down over the mouth of the sexually mature males. As well as this, it has inside its nose a bright red membrane, which it can push out through a nostril and pump up to look like a giant facial whoopee cushion. This blood-coloured balloon can inflate to be bigger than the seal's head and is waved like a peculiar pompom to persuade females to mate with him. The face is typically a solid black in colour, but the rest of the coat is silver, shot through with black spots. The flippers are heavily clawed and the hind flippers, though extremely efficient in the water, are practically useless on land.

Hooded seals spend most of their time alone, coming together only briefly to breed. The pups are born in an exceptionally advanced developmental state, and are weaned after just four days, the shortest lactation period known. Following a short maternal period, the female may mate with an amorous male again almost immediately, before abandoning her pup to its own devices to survive on its fat reserves while on the ice for a few days, prior to diving into the water for the first time. The female can keep a fertilised egg on hold through a process known as delayed implantation, only letting it continue development at a more convenient time.

The indigenous peoples of Greenland and Canada have hunted the hooded seal for hundreds of years, but in the nineteenth and twentieth centuries, hunting increased greatly, with international demand for seal oil and leather and the pelt of cubs. The species has been protected and quotas have been introduced, dictating how many may be hunted, but the population is still shrinking at an alarming rate because of oil spills and pollution. As hooded seals breed on pack ice, global warming could prove disastrous for them.

HOODED SEAL

(Cystophora cristata)

SAGALLA CAECILIAN

(Boulengerula niedeni)

I T OFTEN SEEMS puzzling how evolution can go to all the trouble of creating sophisticated organs like legs, only to misplace them clumsily like a set of keys, a left sock or the Ark of the Covenant. Though at a glance they look like large earthworms, and their scientific name, Gymnophiona, means 'naked snakes', caecilians are actually amphibians. Their closest relatives are frogs and salamanders, though the group diverged from them about 370 million years ago. There are over 200 different types, some of which can grow to be 1.6m long. Most are burrowing creatures but there are a few species in South America that are fully aquatic.

The Sagalla caecilian, which grows to a length of almost 30cm, has strongly pigmented skin, giving it a brownish appearance with a pink-red tinge, and whitish grooves that divide the skin into narrow segments. Like other caecilians, it pushes its way through the soil – using a bony skull which is covered in tough keratin-reinforced skin – in its hunt for termites and worms.

It has two tiny retractable tentacles which might act as tactile feelers or allow the caecilian to pick up chemical cues. When not in use, the tentacles are holstered in small circular holes on each side of the head, between the nostrils and where the eyes aren't! The word 'caecilian' is derived from the Latin word *caecus*, meaning blind. The eyes are not visible but they are there, hidden under a layer of skin and bone, and, though covered, are still capable of distinguishing degrees of light and dark. The mouth is relatively large and contains three rows of

'When not in use, the tentacles are holstered in small circular holes ...'

teeth, two on the upper jaw, and the other one on the lower jaw.

We know that the male Sagalla caecilian fertilises the female internally using a penis-like organ that is an inversion of their cloaca, the posterior opening that serves as the multipurpose opening for the intestinal, reproductive, and urinary tracts. The female then lays her eggs in an underground chamber and guards them until they hatch. Living underground makes the species hard to study and so scientists do their best to infer some of its habits from those of its close relatives. It is thought likely that, as is the case with its relatives, the eggs of the Sagalla caecilian hatch into the adult form without having to go through a larval stage and that the mother feeds them by growing a special nutrient-enriched skin which the hatchlings peel off and eat like the segments of an orange.

The Sagalla caecilian only lives in a small 29km-wide patch of shrubland, at elevations of about 1,000m above sea level, on Sagalla Hill in Kenya. The conversion of land to eucalyptus plantations is altering the soils in that region, making them uninhabitable for the species. Furthermore, the population is being attacked by a fatal chytrid fungus that afflicts amphibians worldwide. It is considered critically endangered.

THIS SHARK IS greatly feared by fish, people and, probably, nails. Growing up to 6m long and having a mouth filled with sharp, jagged teeth, the great hammerhead is certainly capable of inflicting fatal injuries on a human and attacks have been reported. But this tool-headed fish has much more reason to be frightened of us than we have of it: it is persecuted globally. It is actively hunted for its fins for use in shark fin soup. People also use its liver for vitamin supplements, its skin for leather and its meat for fishmeal. Even more destructive than this is the effect of bycatch, the marvellous fish being caught in nets by accident. They can live to be 30 years old and females only breed every two years, having a long gestation period of eleven months. The slow rate of growth and the low number of offspring it produces mean that it is particularly vulnerable to overexploitation and is considered endangered. The great hammerhead is found around the world in warm temperate and tropical waters but migrates towards the poles to chill out during the summer.

Its body is slender and sleek, with a powerful tail and tall, curved, vertical fin; it is only its head, with the eyes splayed out at its outer limits and permanently frowning mouth, that seems out of place. No one is entirely sure why it possesses its mallet-shaped head, but there are many theories, several of which may be true. It is likely that it allows the shark to scan large areas of ocean floor in the search for food. The big head is packed with sensory organs called ampullae of Lorenzini, which pick up physical and chemical changes in the water and even allow the shark to detect the weak electrical signals given off by animals hiding in the sand. They are often among the first sharks to a kill, suggesting that their sense of smell is particularly keen. Some think that the head acts like a rudder and helps the shark manoeuvre at close quarters while chasing nimble fish; or it could help them nail their prey to the sea floor while they deliver a lethal bite.

It feeds on groupers, sea catfish, bony fish, shellfish, squid and other sharks, but its favourite food is stingray. The stingray is a dangerous adversary and the sharks are often found with the poisonous barbs of rays stuck in their mouth or giving them unusual lip piercings.

'No one is entirely sure why it possesses its **mallet-shaped** head, but there are many theories ...'

GREAT HAMMERHEAD

(*Sphyrna mokarran*)

WHEN EVEN CHARLES Darwin, the nature-loving father of the theory of evolution through natural selection, describes a species as 'hideous-looking' and 'most disgusting', then you know it must be truly vile. The Galápagos marine iguana is the world's only marine lizard. They live on the Galápagos Islands in Ecuador where, in the absence of mammalian predators, they have adapted to survive in the harsh environment of the surrounding sea.

Scientists believe that between 10 and 15 million years ago some land-dwelling iguanas from South America must have drifted out to sea on logs or other debris, eventually landing on the Galápagos. From that first species emerged marine iguanas, which, having learnt to swim, quickly spread to nearly all the islands of the archipelago. Each island hosts marine iguanas of unique size, shape and colour.

Looking at its fierce face, razor-sharp teeth, formidable claws and punkish tonsure of spiky scales that runs the length of its spine, you would be surprised to learn that it is a vegetarian, feeding almost exclusively on marine algae in the intertidal zones during low tide. Larger individuals go further afield for their food, diving into the cold water to graze on seaweeds and scrape algae from the surface of deep rocks. They can reach up to 25m below the water's surface. Their spells of swimming must be short, because these cold-blooded creatures need to return to shore and sunbathe to regain heat before taking another dip. Smaller lizards lose heat too quickly to attempt swimming and so stick to gathering food from the rocks. Their food greatly affects their appearance. Their scales are generally grey or black in colour, but during the mating season they may develop blotches of green and red as a result of eating certain seaweeds that bloom in the summer months. As a result of their diet, they consume a great deal of salt, which can be toxic at high levels. To deal with this, they have evolved a nasal gland that allows them to excrete concentrated salt crystals in big, powerful sneezes. The salty snot often lands back on top of their heads, making them look as if they are adorned with a weird white wig.

'... allows them to excrete concentrated salt crystals in big, powerful sneezes.'

Females travel up to 300m inland to lay their eggs in deep burrows that they dig into sand or volcanic ash; burrows that are 30-80cm deep. They often guard the burrows for the first few days but then leave the eggs to finish incubation untended. Unfortunately, introduced species like dogs, cats and rats often destroy these eggs and can decimate a colony's population. This destruction, combined with the effects of oil spills, environmental fluctuations and freak weather events, has led to declining numbers and the Galápagos marine iguana is now classed as vulnerable.

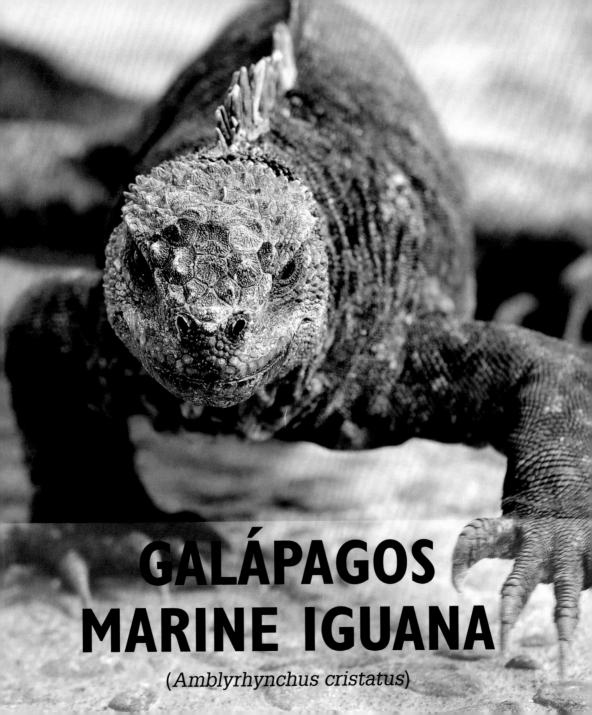

GALÁPAGOS
MARINE IGUANA
(Amblyrhynchus cristatus)

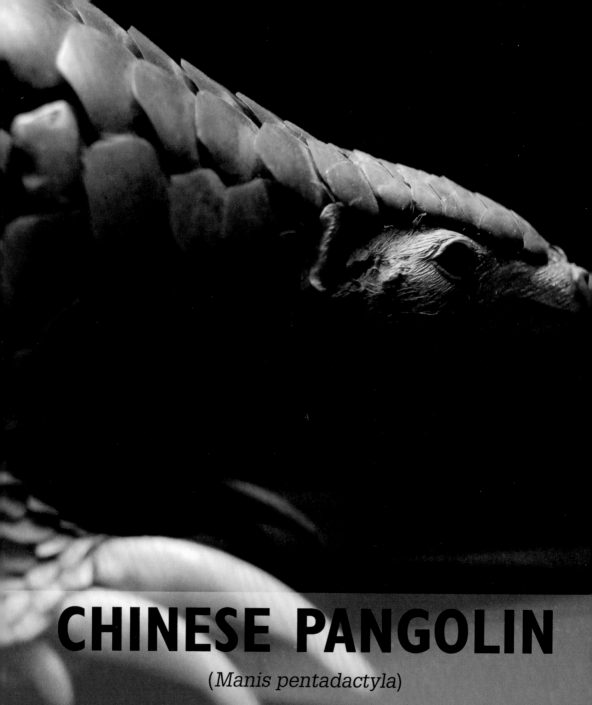

CHINESE PANGOLIN

(Manis pentadactyla)

THE PANGOLIN LOOKS like an anteater dressed as a pine cone. If under attack, it can roll its scaly body into a ball, so that none of its soft flesh is exposed. It is from this behaviour that it got its name: the word pangolin comes from a Malayan word meaning 'the roller'. The bizarre, scaly armour is made from tough keratin.

There are eight species of pangolin, many of which are endangered or near threatened, with the Chinese pangolin being one of the most at risk. It is hunted for its meat and used in traditional, but ineffective, medicines. It lives across a wide variety of habitats, including tropical, coniferous, evergreen and bamboo forests, as well as in grasslands and agricultural fields from India, through China and all the way to Taiwan.

The head is small with tiny, short-sighted eyes; it relies mostly on a strong sense of smell to find its food and can detect the presence of a termite or ant colony from hundreds of metres away.

It uses its claws, which can be up to 5cm long, to tear through soil that can be as hard as concrete and break its way into termite and ant nests. While feeding at the heart of the hive, it protects itself from the retaliating swarm by closing its ears and nostrils. It then flicks at its food with an incredible, thin tongue that can be up to 40cm in length, nearly the length of its body. Once the tongue hits its target, it scoops the prey back into the pangolin's toothless mouth. As it is unable to chew, the meal must be ground down by muscular action in the stomach.

'... an incredible, thin tongue that can be ... nearly the length of its body.'

The Chinese pangolin has a peculiar gait. Struggling with its massive claws, it can slowly wander along on its knuckles or even draw its forelimbs up, claws curled, and rise on its hind legs to walk. Its walk might seem ungainly, but it is both a great climber and a proficient swimmer.

Come autumn, the usually solitary male Chinese pangolins take to sparring over the opportunity to mate with a female. The female will then spend winter in a deep burrow that she excavates near a termite nest for convenient snacking. There, she gives birth to a single offspring, which is weaned underground through the winter, before emerging in spring with its mother, who carries it around on the top of her long, scale-covered tail.

... an anteater dressed as a pine cone.

The common name of the Titicaca water frog is the scrotum frog.

THE **COMMON NAME** of the Titicaca water frog is the scrotum frog. It is so called because of its supremely saggy skin, giving it an appearance reminiscent of perhaps the most unfortunate-looking piece of human anatomy. We can be certain that the comparison is not a flattering one. Having said this, if a man's masculine apparatus is of an olive-green colour, or swollen to the size of a water frog, then he should most definitely seek medical attention.

Those folds of extra skin are what allows the water frog to survive high up in the Andes in Lake Titicaca. The surface of the lake is over 3,800m above sea level. At such an altitude, the air is thinner and there is less oxygen in the water. The Titicaca water frog is the world's largest, fully aquatic frog and though it does have lungs, these are meagre in size and the frog takes up most of its oxygen through its skin. To help with this, the skin's surface area is vast and highly convoluted, helping it extract the maximum oxygen from its environment. When in particularly brackish and stagnant water, it will flap about to move the water over its surface. To aid respiration further, it also has an unusually high red blood cell count, with each individual blood cell being smaller and nimbler, allowing it to flow more easily through the bloodstream to reach tissues.

They used to grow to be huge, weighing over 1kg, making them one of the largest frogs in the world, but unfortunately it has been a long time since anyone has seen one that size. Their numbers are declining because of a large number of factors. Pollution and the large-scale removal of water from the lake for agriculture is killing them, as is the deadly chytridiomycosis fungus, which is afflicting amphibians worldwide. A further pressure is the introduction of invasive, non-native species, with commercially farmed trout posing a particular threat by feasting on tadpoles. But it is not only fish that eat them; it is humans too. There is a belief that eating the aquatic scrotum frog might in some way improve a man's masculinity and so many are stolen from the lake to be made into disgusting frog frappés. This weird broth of liquidised amphibian and spices is believed to improve virility and cure a range of other ailments. There is no scientific basis to this whatsoever and we can only hope it tastes as disgusting as it sounds. Various zoos around the world are trying to breed them in captivity but have so far had only limited success.

TITICACA
WATER FROG
(Telmatobius culeus)

'... up the creek without a paddle.'

LET US HOPE that the American paddlefish is not, somewhat ironically, up the creek without a paddle. It is found across twenty-two states that are part of the Mississippi River basin in the USA. Paddlefish are among the few freshwater fish that filter plankton from the water for their food. The name of the genus, Polyodon, derives from a Greek word meaning 'many tooth' and is a reference to the bony, comb-covered gill arches with which it rakes the water for tiny plankton particles. Its long, ladle-like rostrum is shaped to create lift as the fish swims forward and acts as a stabiliser to hold the head in a steady position. The snout is also peppered with electrosensors that help the paddlefish sense its surroundings and locate prey. They average about 1.5m in length, with males being larger than females. The long body is a uniform, aluminium-grey colour, though paler underneath, and sports a forked and flashy, shark-like tail. Superficially, the species seems to have much in common with sharks, as it lacks scales and has a skeleton mostly made of cartilage rather than bone, but these features are more a result of convergent evolution rather than evidence of an ancestral relationship.

'... sports a *forked* and *flashy*, shark-like tail.'

The breeding season occurs in spring, when large shoals of paddlefish migrate upstream and congregate to spawn. Spawning appears to demand very specific environmental requirements and, therefore, generally only occurs every two to three years. A single female can lay between 300,000 and 600,000 eggs, most of which will die of natural causes. If they make it past their first few years, some may live for up to 55 years, although the average lifespan seems to be around 20 to 30 years.

Paddlefish are closely related to sturgeon and unfortunately are, perhaps, doomed for very similar reasons. As the numbers of caviar-creating sturgeon have fallen, people have turned to paddlefish roe as a substitute, leading to the overexploitation of this species too. On top of being hunted for sport and for their roe, their numbers are also shrinking as a result of interference with their natural habitat, as river systems are altered through damming, sedimentation, pollution and competition from introduced species.

The only other member of the genus is the Chinese paddlefish, which is in even more dire straits. This enormous creature, which can grow up to 7m in length, is one of the largest freshwater fish in the world. It was once common in the Yangtze River, but was last sighted there in 2007. It is listed as critically endangered but, sadly, most biologists think it may already have disappeared completely.

PADDLEFISH

(Polyodon spathula)

ROTI ISLAND SNAKE-NECKED TURTLE

(*Chelodina mccordi*)

BUYING A TURTLENECK pullover to fit this rare reptile would be a tough job. Luckily it already has a shell suit.

The neck of a full-grown Roti Island snake-necked turtle can measure between 7 and 9cm in length, which is as long as its shell. This presents it with an obvious storage problem; it is unable to retract its head into the safety of its shell when in need of protecting itself. Instead it must sling its head backwards along its side and hide it in a gap between the carapace and lower shell to keep safe.

'... a superb *snorkel* ...'

The long neck has several functions. It acts as a superb snorkel, allowing the turtle to breathe, while the rest of its body stays hidden below the water. The turtle can use it to delve into mud on the riverbed, trying to snout out prey. It can even use its neck to make snappy, surprise strikes, snatching food like a viper. It eats snails, prawns, other invertebrates and small fish.

The weirdness of the species has been its downfall and its novel nature has made it one of the most desired turtles in the international pet trade. Even before it was scientifically described, it was so overcollected that the trade was prohibited in 2001, due to the turtle's rarity. Many traders view it as being commercially extinct. We can hope its numbers will increase while no one is out looking for it. It can have up to three breeding periods in a year, giving it a fair chance of recovery.

Females lay clutches of between eight and fourteen eggs, each being about 3cm across and weighing up to 10g. The first tiny hatchlings come after three months, sporting yellow spots on the underside of their shell. The undersides become progressively darker over a few weeks until they are almost black, before doing a decorative U-turn and taking on the pale, fudge-white colour of maturity.

The three remaining populations live in an area of only 70km^2 in the central highlands of Roti Island, Indonesia. Scientists are still debating whether the three populations may even represent genetically distinct subspecies. The snake-necked turtle is still illegally captured, even though it is critically endangered. None of the areas where it lives are currently protected and expanding agricultural developments are impinging on its territory. There is some hope that captive-breeding programs will save this species, but unless serious conservation action is undertaken, it seems likely that it will soon face extinction in the wild.

BALD-HEADED UAKARI

(*Cacajao calvus*)

PERHAPS THE UAKARI is red-faced because it is embarrassed by its bald head. Perhaps it is red-faced with rage because of having its habitat destroyed by logging in the rainforests of Peru and Brazil. More likely, the slapped-looking appearance is a sign of virility, as the redder the monkey's mug, the better its immune system seems to function. Evidence for this comes from observations that individuals suffering from malaria have paler faces and are less likely to find mates. Their scarlet visage is caused by a lack of skin pigments and a vast network of capillaries that run under their facial tissue.

'... the **redder** the monkey's mug, the better its immune system ...'

Not only do they use crimson features to attract mates; they can also deploy an attractive scent from their sternal gland that advertises their availability to members of the opposite sex. The breeding season is between October and May. The mother is pregnant for about six months before giving birth to a single young. She will carry her baby around on her front before, as it grows bigger, transferring it to her back as they roam through the forest. When a male grows old enough, it leaves its natal group and sets out in search of new territories and other females. It is thought to live for approximately 30 years in the wild and has been observed living considerably longer in captivity.

These little monkeys bounce through the treetops in large social groups of up to 100 individuals, searching for seeds, fruit, young buds, flowers, leaves and insects. Troops travel up to 5km a day, defending ranges as large as 600 hectares from rival gangs. A troop will do its best to intimidate opposition using loud vocalisations, ruffling up their hair to appear bigger than they really are and wagging their unusually stubby tails. There are four different subspecies, each of which is attired with differently coloured long, shaggy coats that range from an ash-white to a golden ginger.

The species is considered vulnerable, principally because of the deforestation of its Amazon habitat. As the species is almost entirely arboreal and only ever comes to ground when desperate, it is particularly harmed by logging activities that disrupt the continuity of the canopy and restrict a troop's movement. Even smaller roads can prove impassable boundaries for them. Furthermore, as picky herbivores that eat mostly fruit, they need a large range to find suitable crop-bearing trees. On top of this, they are hunted for their meat or to be used as bait to catch bigger animals.

THE NAME OF this strange Mexican amphibian is thought to come from the Aztec words meaning 'water monster'. One of its oddest characteristics is that it spends its life permanently in the water and, unlike most amphibians, does not undergo a metamorphosis into a more land-based form. It can retain its gills, fins and non-protruding eyes – which lack eyelids and are suited to living underwater – for all its life. This retention of juvenile characteristics into adulthood is known as neoteny or paedomorphosis. Though the axolotl does develop lungs, it doesn't really use them, preferring instead to draw oxygen from its ruff of gills or even from its skin. Biologists have noted that if its habitat dries up, it can metamorphose into a form that will wander off in search of a new home, but that its lifespan seems to suffer by undergoing such a change. The free-living aquatic form can live for up to 12 years. It does have legs, which it uses under the water, leading to its nickname of the 'walking fish'. It grows to a maximum of about 30cm and has tiny teeth that it uses more to grip its food than for chewing.

It has a tiny range, living in only a few lakes and canals around Mexico City. Its natural predators are birds like herons, but it is now being attacked by introduced fish species such as carp as well. The biggest threat, though, comes from a decline in the quality of its habitat due to drainage and pollution.

Conservationists consider the species critically endangered and, though thorough searches of its home range have been made, no specimens have been found for a long time, leading many to think that it may already be extinct in the wild. Fortunately, it is unlikely that the species will go fully extinct as there are so many specimens kept as pets and in laboratories around the world. Scientists study them intently because of their amazing regenerative capabilities. If they lose a limb they can regrow it in a matter of weeks. Rather than developing scar tissue, they form a 'bud' of stem cells at the end of the damaged appendage, from which a new limb will grow without any evidence of harm whatsoever. They can even regenerate and repair portions of the brain and spine. The precise mechanisms are still not understood but scientists hope that, through studying this weird little amphibian, they may be able to reverse engineer some medical techniques that will allow us better to repair our body.

'If they lose a *limb* they can regrow it in a matter of weeks.'

AXOLOTL
(*Ambystoma mexicanum*)

RED-HEADED VULTURE

(Sarcogyps calvus)

*'Vultures get a **bad rap** that they don't deserve.'*

PERHAPS THE ADVANTAGE of having a bald and bright red head is that, when it is smeared in blood and rank decaying remains, it doesn't look any worse. The red-headed vulture, sometimes known as the Asian king vulture or Indian black vulture, is a medium-sized Old World vulture. It has a wingspan of over 2m, a black body with a pale grey band at the base of its flight feathers and a naked head flanked by two fleshly flaps, like earrings made of bacon, that hang down each side of its face.

'... like watching a very **bloody** *soap opera ...'*

Vultures get a bad rap that they don't deserve. While we admire the vicious lethality of carnivores like lions, scavengers are, unfairly, seen as lazy. Vultures are like the binmen of the natural world and play an essential part in the process of nutrient recycling. Without them, parts of the world would be rife with stinking corpses. Observing vultures at a kill is like watching a very bloody soap opera; the various species play subtly different roles in their butchery. Larger species, with stronger, more cleaver-like beaks, have to be the first to begin the dissection of the corpse, acting almost like a tin opener, before any of the other species can get stuck in to the feast. The red-headed vulture is seldom first in the pecking, or in this case, dismembering order. Larger vultures of the gyps genus often chase them from a corpse.

The red-headed vulture was once widespread throughout the Indian sub-continent and South-east Asia, but in recent decades it has undergone significant declines in both range and population and so has been classed as critically endangered. The populations of many Asian vulture species have been crashing since the 1990s, at least in part due to the widespread use of the veterinary medicine Diclofenac to treat livestock in India. Vultures eat the carcasses of livestock that have been treated with the drug and are poisoned by the accumulation of the chemical in their bodies. They lack the enzyme needed to break the compound down and so are killed by it. It is estimated that there has been a decline in numbers of vultures on the Indian sub-continent of up to 95 per cent. Fortunately, the manufacture of Diclofenac has now been banned in India, Nepal and Pakistan and there are captive-breeding programs in action. To help bolster populations in Cambodia, the World Wildlife Fund runs regular 'vulture restaurants': feeding stations which allow researchers both to feed and monitor visiting vultures.

YANGTZE GIANT
SOFTSHELL TURTLE

(Rafetus swinhoei)

THOUGH IT RESEMBLES a bloated and battered old leather suitcase, the Yangtze giant softshell turtle is a living legend. Unfortunately, the legends that surround it are probably not true and the chance of the species staying alive is slim at best. Tragically, there are thought to be only four individuals in existence and three of them are male. This makes this not just one of the most endangered turtles in the world, but one of the most endangered life forms, full stop. It is a truly massive creature that can weigh over 120kg, with a shell that can be larger than 1m. It feeds on fish, crabs, snails, water hyacinth, frogs, and leaves.

'… a bloated and battered old leather **suitcase** *…'*

One male specimen, located in Hoan Kiem Lake in Hanoi, is believed by many who live near the lake to be the legendary Golden Turtle God, Kim Qui. He is supposed to have appeared at opportune moments throughout Vietnamese history and furnished warrior heroes with mystical weaponry, including a magic crossbow and an unbeatable sword known as Heaven's Will, which was used in the fight for Vietnam's independence from China. The story has made this individual a national emblem and granted it a special celebrity status that has ensured its survival there.

In 2011 it was found to have sores on its back and legs and was attended to by a group of about fifty rescuers, while thousands of people crowded around the lake to see it treated. This turtle is lucky: in the past they were hunted for food, folk medicine and as trophies.

Another male lives a solitary existence in a lake west of the city, while the other two turtles are safe in captivity in Suzhou Zoo, China. Having lived in separate facilities for many years, the male and last female were brought together in 2008 in the hope of them breeding. Eggs have been produced each year since, but all have died during incubation. Scientists are doing their best to try to improve the chances of procreation. They noticed that the first eggs produced had a very thin shell and so started feeding the pair on specially made sausages with a high calcium content to help improve the quality of the eggs. It has also been feared that they may have been eating litter dropped by careless zoo visitors and so their enclosure has since been surrounded by glass barriers.

Another possible reason for the struggle to conceive could be the advanced age of the male, which could well be over 100 years old. Biologists in the area of the Red River are always on the lookout for individuals in the wild that they may not know about and are considering capturing the last-known males in the hope that they might make a more reproductively successful match with the female.

'… one of the most **endangered** *life forms …'*

THE SLOTHS MUST be the only animals that are named after a deadly sin. There are six different species and all of them have turned laziness into a survival strategy. They spend almost all of their lives in trees, just hanging out, relaxing and taking it easy. Their metabolic rate is less than half that of other similarly sized mammals, allowing them to survive on very little food. Everything they do, they do slowly. They move only about 38m a day and spend up to fifteen hours each day napping. They feed almost exclusively on leaves and twigs, nipping off food using their hard lips and grinding it up with continuously growing teeth. They process the food slowly by means of a long, multi-chambered stomach that is filled with cellulose-digesting bacteria that help break down cell walls and make the most of their difficult diet. They use their long arms and claws to hang upside down in a hammock-like posture near the crowns of trees, slowly moving into and out of the light to help control their body temperature. They spend so much of their life upside down that many of their internal organs are in different positions when compared with those of their other mammalian cousins. The long arms make them capable of a strong front crawl and they are surprisingly good swimmers.

*'... the only animals that are named after a **deadly sin**.'*

*'There is an entire ecosystem that lives within their **fuzz** ...'*

The maned three-toed sloth, so named because of the ring of black hairs that surrounds its neck and runs down its shoulders, is one of the rarest forms of sloth and is only found in Brazil. Its body is covered in coat of long, shaggy hairs that grow from the stomach to the back, the opposite direction to hair growth in most mammals, allowing rainwater to run off it more easily. The hair is a caramel-brown colour but often seems to be tinted green thanks to the presence of algae that grow among the hairs. The algae are thought to aid the camouflage of the creature, helping it to blend in more with its surroundings, but more recent research has suggested that the sloth might even be eating some of this algae and so is perhaps farming on its own fur. There is an entire ecosystem that lives within their fuzz, including the highly specialised sloth moth, which may help the sloth maintain its algal garden. The algae are likely passed on from mother to child during the baby's development as it clings to its mother. Females normally bear only one baby every year, but sometimes sloths' low level of movement means that it takes longer than that for a male and female to find each other. This slow rate of reproduction and the destruction of their habitat have combined to make this species vulnerable.

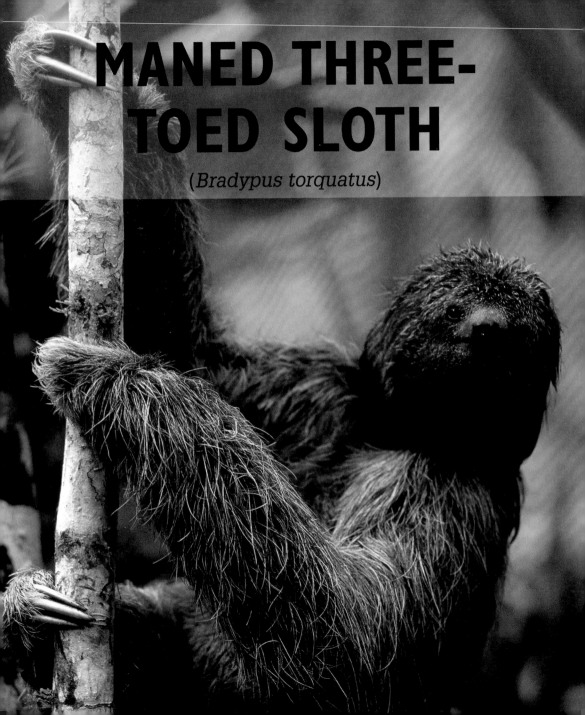

MANED THREE-TOED SLOTH

(*Bradypus torquatus*)

MANY CONSIDER THIS endangered animal from Australasia to be the deadliest bird on the planet. It can be ferocious; you should not let its peculiar appearance fool you. Just because it looks like a dapper ostrich, sporting a technicolour throat and a fez-like cask that often sits atop its head at a jaunty angle, this does not mean it isn't dangerous.

Though the word cassowary loosely translates from Papuan as 'horned head', the precise purpose of the cask is unknown. It is too soft and spongy to afford much protection, but it may help deflect branches as it runs through the forest or it may protect the head from falling fruit.

The cassowary is a member of the ratite family, a group of birds that includes the biggest of birds, the ostrich, as well as the emu, the two kinds of rhea and the smallest and cutest member of the family, the little ball of feathers that is the kiwi. None of these species can fly but some of them are amazing runners. A cassowary's strong legs allow it to sprint through the jungle at up to 50km per hour and make huge leaps of up to 1.5m. The legs also give it a fearsome kick which, when coupled with claws like switchblades, make it capable of eviscerating anyone who dares stand in its way. Because of these claws, people often used to describe cassowaries as being like feathered velociraptors. The comparison is a bad one: for a start, recent fossil finds have led us to believe that most, if not all, raptor dinosaurs were covered with feathers. Furthermore the vicious velociraptor that features in films was, in reality, probably only the size of a chicken, making it so much less intimidating than any cassowary. However, in spite of being separated by millions of years, they do still have surprisingly similar feet.

Fortunately for us though, the cassowary is not out to get us: instead, it is a shy frugivore that feasts mostly on berries. Its meals play a pivotal role in the rainforest ecosystem: as the cassowary wanders around, pooping as it travels, it helps distribute the seeds of many fruit.

The female lays her eggs directly onto the forest floor and from that point the male takes sole responsibility for them. The male incubates the eggs for around fifty days, turning and tending them, only ever leaving in order to drink. The eggs hatch into small creatures like roadrunners, with black and yellow go-faster stripes. The male will care for his offspring for up to sixteen months, even shielding them under his tail if they are threatened. Feisty though this beast might be, it will never win a fight with a car, and, unfortunately, traffic accidents are killing a great many of them.

*'... it looks like a **dapper** ostrich, sporting a technicolour throat and a **fez-like** cask ...'*

SOUTHERN CASSOWARY

(*Casuarius casuarius*)

GHARIAL

(Gavialis gangeticus)

THE GHARIAL GETS its name from the knobbly nose of the male: the bulbous blemish that adorns the tip of the male's snout is said to resemble an Indian earthenware pot called a 'ghara'. The precise purpose of the 'pot' is unknown but many believe that it may play a role as a resonator, producing a loud, buzzing noise during vocalisation and sexual display, or that it may act as a visual signal of masculinity to help entice females to mate with him.

> '... the *bulbous* blemish that adorns the tip of the male's snout ...'

The gharial is one of the biggest of the crocodilians – a family that contains true crocodiles, alligators and caimans – being able to grow to 6m and weigh over 160kg. In spite of being so large, its snout is much narrower than that of its broad-jawed cousins. It may be comparatively dainty but it comes packed with dangerous, razor-sharp, needle-like teeth.

While most crocodiles feed upon animals that come to the river's edge to drink, the gharial eats mostly fish and other creatures that are more at home in the water. As a result, its mouth has evolved to be able to swish through the water with greater ease to try to spike fast-swimming fish on its interlocking teeth. It herds fish, using its body to corral them against the shore, and stuns its targets using its underwater jaw clap. Like all crocodilians, gharials are incapable of chewing and must swallow their prey whole or in torn-up pieces. Their jaws are too delicate to tackle larger prey and any reports describing them as man-eaters are sensationalist nonsense. Their whole body is streamlined to help them swim and they even have partially webbed feet. They struggle when on land, being unable to walk in the semi-upright stance adopted by other crocodilians; they prefer to slalom along on their belly through the mud to their basking sites. They like to live in flowing rivers with deep pools that have high sand banks and good fish stocks.

The numbers of gharials seem to have crashed by over 95 per cent since the 1950s and the species is considered critically endangered. The drastic decline can be attributed to a variety of causes, including over-hunting for skins and trophies, egg collection for consumption, killing for indigenous medicine, and killing by fishermen. Though hunting has become much less common in recent years, the destruction of their habitat by pollution and mismanagement is harming the populations still further. Conservation efforts are underway to help care for their nesting sites and protect their habitat.

> '... any reports describing them as *man-eaters* are *sensationalist* nonsense.'

GASTRIC-BROODING FROG

(*Rheobatrachus*)

THOUGH TRAGIC, THE story of the gastric-brooding frog, one of the world's weirdest and most awesome amphibians, is one of hope.

It became famous shortly after its discovery in 1972 because of its novel, faintly cannibalistic and rather gross means of reproduction. After laying her frogspawn and having it fertilized externally by a male, the mother greedily gobbles it up, swallowing the next generation whole. It sounds like species suicide, but no. The jelly coating of the eggs contains a hormone which switches off the production of stomach acid so that the eggs are not broken down and digested. Weeks later the eggs hatch into tadpoles which then develop into tiny froglets and the mother gives birth through her mouth, vomiting her children into the world.

'... *vomiting* her children into the world.'

There were two species of gastric-brooding frog found in Queensland Australia. Please note the use of the past tense there. The tragedy is that both species have died out: factors including, pollution, invasive species, killer fungal pathogens and habitat destruction have been blamed for their demise. None have been seen in the wild since 1984 and most conservationists consider it completely extinct.

But the story does not end there. A team in Australia, known as the Lazarus Project, has ambitions to bring it back from the dead by cloning. So far they have managed to produce a batch of living, viable embryos. Looking down their microscopes, scientists have watched the cells divide and divide again and then reach a point where they stop. The next step will be to overcome this hurdle and produce eggs that will hatch into tadpoles and can be nurtured until they become adult frogs, capable of reproducing by themselves using the much more traditional method of sex, swallowing and then being sick.

This is not the first such attempt at de-extinction. The Pyrenees ibex, a kind of Spanish mountain goat, died out in 2000, but scientists managed to salvage some DNA from skin samples and, using a domestic goat as a surrogate mother, succeeded in cloning a long-gone female ibex, bringing the species back from the dead. Unfortunately the individual died after seven minutes due to complications with its lungs, making this the only species to have gone extinct twice.

This might seem a somewhat backwards approach to conservation, focusing on resurrecting species rather than on protecting those that are still surviving, but in the fight to preserve biodiversity, every tool has a place. Zoologists have already started gathering the DNA of organisms; freezing a mere few grams of tissue with liquid nitrogen to preserve it for study. These frozen samples represent more than just an opportunity for research but may, in the worst case scenario, act as a genetic ark, allowing us to clone lost species and, eventually, reintroduce them into the wild.

ABOUT THE AUTHOR

SIMON WATT IS a biologist, writer, science communicator and presenter. He runs 'Ready Steady Science', a science communication company committed to making information interesting and takes science-based performances into schools, museums, theatres and festivals. He has worked on science-inspired theatre productions which have toured nationally, performed stand-up comedy about science and natural history, created resources and events for some of the UK's most loved museums and cultural establishments including the Natural History Museum and the Science Museum, written dozens of articles for national newspapers including *The Times*, *The Sunday Times* and *The Independent* and is a regular contributor on radio and TV. He is perhaps best known as a presenter on the BAFTA-winning documentary series *Inside Nature's Giants* and the Channel 4 special *The Elephant: Life After Death*.

www.readysteadyscience.com
@simondwatt

FURTHER READING

AMPHIBIAN SURVIVAL ALLIANCE

The Amphibian Survival Alliance protects amphibians and their habitats through dynamic partnerships worldwide.

www.amphibians.org

ARKive

ARKive maintain an amazing website choc-a-bloc full of information about the wildlife of the world including photos and film media.

www.arkive.org

EDGE

The EDGE of Existence programme highlights and conserves one-of-a-kind species that are on the verge of extinction. They are based at the Zoological Society of London (ZSL).

www.edgeofexistence.org

THE IUCN RED LIST OF THREATENED SPECIES

The International Union for the Conservation of Nature (IUCN) is, among other things, trying to document and analyse the populations of the world's species to try and understand how we might best help endangered species.

www.iucnredlist.org

TURTLE SURVIVAL ALLIANCE

The Turtle Survival Alliance (TSA) formed in 2001 in response to the Asian Turtle Crisis. It has since become a recognised force in turtle and tortoise conservation globally and hopes to end turtle extinction.

www.turtlesurvival.org

WORLD LAND TRUST

World Land Trust (WLT) is an international conservation charity, which protects the world's most biologically important and threatened habitats acre by acre. It has funded partner organisations around the world to create reserves, and give permanent protection to habitats and wildlife.

www.worldlandtrust.org

WORLD WILDLIFE FUND

The World Wide Fund for Nature (WWF) is an international non-governmental organisation that protects endangered wildlife and environments, tackles climate change and promotes sustainable use of resources.

www.wwf.org.uk

PICTURE CREDITS

p. 35, shoebill, © AP Photo/Itsuo Inouye/Press Association

p. 37, big-headed turtle, © Press Association

p. 39, pink underwing moth, © Lui Weber/Rex Features

p. 40, dugong, © AP Photo/Linda Lombardi/Press Association

p. 42, long-wattled umbrellabird, © Murray Cooper/Minden Pictures/FLPA

p. 45, hagfish, © AAP Image/Massey University/Press Association

p. 47, dromedary jumping-slug, © Kristiina Ovaska

p. 49, Tonkin snub-nosed monkey, © Xi Zhinong/Minden Pictures/FLPA

p. 50, southern ground-hornbill, © Press Association

p. 53, largetooth sawfish, © Oceans-Image/Photoshot

p. 55, flightless dung beetle, © Press Association

p. 56, ghost bat, © David Hosking

p. 59, California condor, © Press Association

p. 61, humphead wrasse, © Imago/Photoshot

p. 62, giant Gippsland earthworm, © NHPA/Photoshot

p. 65, eastern long-beaked echidna, © AP Photo/Conservation International, Stephen Richards, HO/Press Association

p. 67, Myers' Surinam toad, © Dein Freund der Baum, Wikimedia Commons

p. 69, bumphead parrotfish, © AP Photo/Keith A. Ellenbogen/Press Association

p. 70, blue-gray tail-dropper slug, © Kristiina Ovaska

p. 72, Cuban solenodon, © Photo Researchers/FLPA

p. 75, olm, © Wild Wonders of Europe/ Hodalic/naturepl.com

p. 77, razorback sucker, © Everett/Photoshot

p. 78, Lord Howe Island stick insect, © AAP Image/Joe Castro/Press Association

p. 80, Sulawesi babirusa, © Press Association

p. 82, Chinese giant salamander, © NHPA/Photoshot

p. 85, blobfish, © NORFANZ/Photoshot

p. 87, Chinese water deer, © William Warby, Wikimedia Commons

p. 89, purple pig-nosed frog, © Sachin Rai, www.landofthewild.com

p. 90, Pacific lamprey, © AP Photo/Rick Bowmer/Press Association

p. 93, Dracula ant, © April Nobile, www.AntWeb.org

p. 95, spotted handfish, © NHPA/Photoshot

p. 96, Saiga antelope, © Photo Researchers/FLPA

p. 99, Chinhai spiny newt, © Dr Jiang Jianping

p. 100, beluga, © AP Photo/Nicolae Dumitrache/Press Association

p. 102, prickly redfish, © François Michonneau, Wikimedia Commons

p. 105, hooded seal, © Doug Allan/naturepl.com

p. 106, sagalla caecilian, © Dr John Measey

p. 109, great hammerhead, © Oceans Image/Photoshot

p. 111, Galápagos marine iguana, © Press Association

p. 112, Chinese pangolin, © AP Photo/Seth Wenig/Press Association

p. 115, Titicaca water frog, © Pete Oxford/naturepl.com

p. 117, paddlefish, © Oceans-Image/Photoshot

p. 118, Roti Island snake-necked turtle, © ZSSD/Minden Pictures/FLPA

p. 120, bald-headed uakari, © Evgenia Kononova, Wikimedia Commons

p. 123, axolotl, © Jan-Peter Kasper dpa/lth/Press Association

p. 124, red-headed vulture, © Press Association

p. 126, Yangtze giant softshell turtle, © Gerald Kuchling/Turtle Survival Alliance (TSA)

p. 129, maned three-toed sloth, © NHPA/Photoshot

p. 131, southern cassowary, © Press Association

p. 132, gharial, © AP Photo/Tony Dejak/Press Association

p. 134, gastric-brooding frog, © NHPA/Photoshot